"*The Trials and Passion of Christ* reads as easily as a series of sermons and is written by one who clearly has a pastor's heart for relating the Word to life for the sake of encouraging discipleship."
—DANIEL M. BELL JR.
Lutheran Theological Southern Seminary

"*The Trials and Passion of Christ* brings you into the presence of each event as they unfold. Michael Cannon has written an insightful and inspiring treasure that will benefit Christians all over the world. His approach makes it easy to follow and allows the reader to gain tremendous revelation of John 18 and 19. This book should be used by ministers, adult class teachers, and Bible teachers. I highly recommend this book and I can't wait to get my copy!"
—ALBERT L. DOWNING
Senior Pastor, Oak Grove Baptist Church
Pontiac, South Carolina

"Mike Cannon's *The Trials and Passion of Christ* is a wonderful study of our Lord's last moments on earth. His down to earth stories are those that many readers can relate to. I was able to close my human eyes and see the examples via 'spiritual eyes.' The study will be valuable to any minister preparing for sermons or Bible studies during the days leading up to our Lord's triumph over the grave and death. Any reader will be inspired by Jesus' suffering endured on our behalf. I strongly recommend this work."
—SAMUEL J. T. BOONE
Chaplain (Colonel) USA—Retired

The Trials and Passion of Christ

The Trials and Passion of Christ

An Expository and Analytical Commentary on John 18 and 19

MICHAEL CANNON JR.

RESOURCE *Publications* • Eugene, Oregon

THE TRIALS AND PASSION OF CHRIST
An Expository and Analytical Commentary on John 18 and 19

Copyright © 2011 Michael Cannon Jr. All rights reserved. Except for brief quotations in critical publications or reviews, no part of this book may be reproduced in any manner without prior written permission from the publisher. Write: Permissions, Wipf and Stock Publishers, 199 W. 8th Ave., Suite 3, Eugene, OR 97401.

Resource Publications
An Imprint of Wipf and Stock Publishers
199 W. 8th Ave., Suite 3
Eugene, OR 97401

www.wipfandstock.com

ISBN 13: 978-1-60899-877-7

Manufactured in the U.S.A.

For Bevalie
Always and Forever

Contents

Foreword by Gordon Reed / xi

1. Jesus isn't Hard to Find / 1
2. Judas the Friend of Jesus / 10
3. Arrested / 19
4. The Inquisition / 29
5. Peter's Denial / 38
6. The Jewish Trial / 49
7. Jesus the Outlaw / 60
8. Once a King / 69
9. Uncomprehended Truth / 80
10. Barabbas / 88
11. He Suffered Under Pontius Pilate / 95
12. Via Dolorosa / 105
13. King of the World / 115
14. Prophetic Fulfillment / 123
15. The Love of a Son / 133
16. I Thirst / 139
17. The Sixth Word from the Cross / 146
18. Pierced / 155
19. Buried with the King / 162

Bibliography / 171

Foreword

Michael Cannon, Pastor of Cliffwood Presbyterian Church in Augusta Georgia, and Army Chaplain is also a gifted writer and astute student and Preacher of the Word of God. His latest commentary is on the Passion of Christ as depicted in the Gospel of John, Chapters 18-19. In this well written book, Rev. Cannon describes the passion of Christ as if he had been an eye witness to these crucial events in the redeeming work of our Lord. He does this in such a way that as you read this work, you find yourself in the role of an eye witness, too!

While he is obviously well read in the works of many others, including the Biblical scholarship of the reformation, and the post reformation era, he also has a refreshing originality in this work. He has the rare ability to combine the best of scholarship with an intensely practical and edifying commentary that not only challenges the mind, but also warms the heart. His questions which he forces us to face are also very convicting. One example of this is seen in his analysis of Judas' treachery. He forces us to examine our own hearts to see if we can detect in us some of the same sins which led up to the ultimate sin of Judas' betrayal of Christ.

Through this book and others he has written and will write he extends his pastor–teacher role beyond the confines of the local church and even the broader vistas of the chaplaincy. Having seen something of the good results of his patient and thorough teaching and discipling of his immediate congregation, I have good hope that all who read this book will also benefit from it and grow in their likeness to the Lord Jesus as Michael Cannon has so obviously done himself.

Gordon Reed

1

Jesus Isn't Hard to Find

John 18:1–11

When Jesus had spoken these words, he went out with his disciples across the Kidron Valley, where there was a garden, which he and his disciples entered. Now Judas, who betrayed him, also knew the place, for Jesus often met there with his disciples. So Judas, having procured a band of soldiers and some officers from the chief priests and the Pharisees, went there with lanterns and torches and weapons.

Then Jesus, knowing all that would happen to him, came forward and said to them, "Whom do you seek?" They answered him, "Jesus of Nazareth." Jesus said to them, "I am he." Judas, who betrayed him, was standing with them. When Jesus said to them, "I am he," they drew back and fell to the ground. So he asked them again, "Whom do you seek?" And they said, 'Jesus of Nazareth.' Jesus answered, "I told you that I am he. So, if you seek me, let these men go." This was to fulfill the word that he had spoken: "Of those whom you gave me I have lost not one." Then Simon Peter, having a sword, drew it and struck the high priest's servant and cut off his right ear. (The servant's name was Malchus.) So Jesus said to Peter, "Put your sword into its sheath; shall I not drink the cup that the Father has given Me?"

The record of the Passion of John complements the other gospels. However, you'll find the record of the Passion in John is a little bit different from the Synoptics simply because John provides additional details which are omitted by the others, and likewise, the Synoptics, that is, Matthew, Mark, and Luke, provide details omitted by John.

We might ask, Why the difference? Why the apparent disparity? Why is it John would leave out, for example, the details of Gethsemane, which feature so prominently in the other gospels? Each writer has his own purpose. Matthew, first of all, presents Christ as King of the Jews, and so he often writes as to portray Christ in that kingly role. Mark presents Jesus to us as the great Servant Prophet who comes to do the will of the Father, while Luke presents him as the Servant Son of Man. In fact, Luke presents Christ as the perfect Son of Man who gave his life for us, the Prophet who comes to do the will of the Father.

John, on the other hand, keeps a very high Christology, showing that Jesus is the divine, incarnate Word of God. He keeps Jesus' eternal son-ship and his authority over all things before us. So in John 18:1–11, a description not mentioned in the Synoptics is that when Jesus spoke, all of those who had come to arrest him fell backwards, showing even in the moment of his arrest, Jesus was exercising his power because he is God in every situation, that he is not overcome or overwhelmed by any.

While the other writers describe the trial before the Sanhedrin, John chooses instead to record Jesus' examination in the house of Annas. John omits the transfiguration and institution of the Lord's supper as well as the agony of Jesus in Gethsemane; those will be in the Synoptics.

Perhaps due to John's high theology, the French commentator, Frédéric Godet, sees three points emerging and characterizing the Passion narrative of John. And they've been the tone throughout the Gospel of John. The first is that *Jesus causes his glory to shine through circumstances.* No matter the circumstance, because Jesus has been placed in the sovereignty of God, his glory has shown forth. Whether he was being challenged by Pharisees or Sadducees, or whether he was ministering by teaching the disciples, his glory always shines forth. Throughout the high priestly prayer in John 17, it was Christ's glory which was set before us.

The second feature of John's book is that *the Jewish unbelief manifests itself as a dark and morally perverse agent working against the will of God.* Over and over again as Christ performs a function that can only be described as "of the Lord," the Pharisees and the Sadducees continue to plot in their moral perversity against the work of God as it is found in Christ Jesus. And then finally, the third significant theme which we find throughout the Gospel of John is *the faith of the disciples continues to grow even through trial and even in dark time;, this growing faith of God's people is apparent even when they are facing temptation and difficulty.*

In verse 1 of Chapter 18, we read, "When Jesus had spoken these words . . . ." Various commentators will take this all the way back to chapter 14. But it is sufficient to say when Jesus had finished this high priestly prayer, he had also finished wrapping up any ministry which the disciples would hear from his own lips before he set his face to the cross. He never swerved left and he never swerved right. Thus John deliberately records that, "When Jesus had spoken these words, he went out with his disciples across the Kidron Valley."

Let it not escape us that Jesus did not delay. He did not procrastinate. He did not begin a new conversation. There was no looking in any other direction; when he finished these words, Jesus knew the next place for him to go would be to the garden where he would be betrayed. He was consecrated to his purpose, and so he headed east across the slopes of the Kidron Valley which fall about 200 feet below the base of the temple's court. On the slopes of the Kidron Valley, you'll find the Mount of Olives.

The name *Kidron* means *dark and turbid*. It's a difficult, dark place. In fact, the water in the river that runs there typically is not even present in the summer; it's only in the winter when there is snow and cold that there is water in the river. And the water, because of the nature of that valley, was always dark water. Additionally, in the seasons of temple sacrifice, the blood from all of the animals would drain from the temple down into the Kidron Valley and into the river making the water even darker. The Kidron Valley—a dark and foreboding place, but the location of the Mount of Olives.

Other gospels tell of Gethsemane and the anguish of our Savior in those last hours. The Mount of Olives or Gethsemane itself is often translated as *oil press*. An oil press, which would have been located in the Garden of Gethsemane, where that juice of the olives would be pressed out, there our Savior would go. And there in a time of prayer our Savior would be pressed by the stresses and the tensions he in his humanity was about to face. Just as the oil is drained and pressed out of the olives, blood would pour forth from our Savior's brow. And in that time of pressure and in that time of being pressed in the Garden of Gethsemane, he prayed unto the Lord, "O My Father, if it be possible, let this cup pass from me: nevertheless not as I will, but as thou wilt."

The cup of the Lord in this dark place, the Kidron Valley, reminds us of Poe's poem, *The Raven* when he says, "Deep into that darkness peering, long I stood there wondering, fearing, / doubting, dreaming dreams no mortal ever dared to dream before." Such a dark, such a foreboding place, this Kidron Valley—and there Jesus, who takes only three with him to pray with him—and they keep falling asleep—prays alone in his anguish, and he prays that if it was the Father's will that this cup would pass from him.

What cup? What cup is our Lord talking about? A cup of divine judgment which is filled with God's wrath against sin. We find it in several places—two of them, Psalm, 11, verse 6, "Let him rain coals on the wicked; fire and sulfur and a scorching wind shall be the portion of their cup," or Psalm 75:8, "For in the hand of the LORD there is a cup with foaming wine, well mixed, and he pours out from it, and all the wicked of the earth shall drain it down to the dregs." Our Lord says, "Father if it could be according to your will, may this cup pass from me; but nevertheless, not my will, but yours be done." In times of trouble we often fall back. We avoid difficult times.

During a drive to church a couple of weeks ago on the newly opened stretch of 520, my wife noticed that dark clouds were gathering ahead of us. We still had clear skies in front of us, but dark clouds were gathering, and there seemed almost to be a wall between the clear sky and the dark clouds. So dark were they and so dark was the landscape under the clouds that it did send a bit of a chill into us because of the stark contrast between the clear skies which we were in and the dark clouds that were ahead, so much so that she even encouraged me to perhaps take another route instead of driving into the dark clouds. It seemed that wall of darkness was gobbling up, consuming the clear space that was before it.

After our Lord's prayer to the Father, through which he raised up the high and grand themes of hope, and victory, and a continuing ministry, the dark cloud of Calvary begins to obscure the view of the promises that had been foretold. It's a dark cloud neither he nor we can go around. We must pass through darkness in life. We must pass through because victory is not by going around, but by going through the troubled waters of Calvary. As we step into the dark path of Gethsemane, let us keep as the meditation of our heart Romans 8:28, all things work together "for those who are called according to his purpose."

Everything in the story that follows would seem to be tragic. Sometimes in literature you may call this a comedy. I've never really understood that phrase because there is rarely anything funny about a comedy. It's a riches-to-rags or rags-to-riches-to-rags story. Here Jesus, who had been transfigured and shown forth in his glory, who had been proven by his teaching and his miracles to be the Son of God, would now face a humiliating death. Everything from this point, as we go into Gethsemane and on to the resurrection, is tragic. A friend will betray his mentor, an innocent man will be arrested, justice will be forfeited for political and self-ambition for political gain, and an innocent man will be murdered. But John will show us that even in the injustice, Jesus will be glorified.

In their pursuit of self-interest, the Jewish moral blindness will be made clear. And because of God's sovereign hand and Christ's glory, the apostles will grow in their faith and commitment. For the believer, dark days lead to glory. But for the unbeliever, dark days are only a sign of their own end which lies before them. This is a perspective we want to learn and keep before us as we journey through the Passion of Christ.

We want to dwell for just a moment on these introductory verses in this valley of Kidron where Christ has now gone. We want to consider the context in which Christ now found himself before we begin our journey in earnest because in that darkness and in that foreboding place our Savior journeyed. He stepped into the darkness, he stepped into the foreboding place, he went into the garden on the Mount of Olives knowing it was in that very place he would be betrayed. He did not go around, he did not turn himself in, he went there to be betrayed and to be taken in to trial in the dark of night, to be beaten and humiliated and crucified in a mock trial.

We want to keep that perspective as we journey through this Passion of Christ because while the Christian may experience tragedy, we find in the Passion of Christ ultimately there is really no tragedy for one who is in Christ. We will suffer. In fact, suffering is a part of our calling to serve Christ. We are to take up our cross; we are to undergo the baptism which Jesus himself has undergone. But the days of suffering aren't to end in tragedy because they work to build us in the faith and push us on towards Christ-likeness.

But how do most of us think of suffering? How do most of us consider the dark valleys when we journey into the Kidron Valley ourselves? Do we consider it a work of the Divine? Do we consider it God's providence when we struggle in times of suffering, or do we try to fit suffering into some sort of a work of sovereignty that keeps us thinking along two lines where we think God has his world and suffering does not belong to that world and therefore God is indifferent at best to our suffering. Although he will preserve our lives, the suffering remains our own perhaps even because the work of our own hand.

We think sometimes with two minds. Is it to guard our orthodox thinking and so we avoid any attempt to reconcile life to our God and to theology? The result is a God who is removed from life and a God who will rarely lead us into prayer. How can we pray to a God who is so far removed from real life? And what interest do we have in theology when theology would have so little to do with real life? And so we have a God who is there, whom we believe in and whom we worship, but a God who is just there and we are left here to work through the issues of life. And so we end up double-minded and our lives will begin to reflect it.

Some see struggle as orchestrated by God, not that he's far removed, but that God himself causes trouble because like a composer, he's organizing a grand symphony of life that sounds forth his glory. And in doing that they see this great conductor of a great orchestral piece as One who is manipulating life and history and causing suffering only so that he may be glorified in the removal of suffering. This leads us to believe that God is waiting for us to live right, so we pray, so we get right, expecting him to remove our suffering and trouble. Now we have a God who is near but one who seems random and impersonal in his treatment of us.

Others just ignore difficult times and look forward to eternity. They just pretend it doesn't happen. They smile and say, "Oh it just doesn't matter. These things don't matter." They have no expectation for anything but hardship in this life and so there is a bit of a fatalistic approach as they say, "It doesn't matter what happens in this life as long as I get to heaven in the end."

Now there may be elements in each of these that, not taken to the extreme, could be considered to be somewhat true. We can acknowledge after reading John 9 that affliction can be used for God's glory. There we found a man who was born blind and Jesus' explanation to the man was that God had caused him to be blind so he would be healed for God's own glory. It wasn't blindness because of the man's sin or unrighteousness; it was for God's own glory. So we do acknowledge there are times when God causes life and history to work for his own glory. We also acknowledge we aren't in heaven yet and that there will be suffering and dark times in this life while we are journeying on towards our heavenly destination.

But are these are our only way of thinking through hardship in this life, to come up with some rational explanation, to just somehow set it all aside rationally? Is that the example we see in Christ? As Christ goes into the Garden of Gethsemane and prays to the Father, is he saying, "Lord, I know you are occupied with the things of heaven and that the suffering I have down here is my own, but if you have found me to be righteous, Father, somehow remove the suffering?" No, he doesn't. He sees his suffering infolded and incorporated into the plan of God for God's own glory. Thus he says, "Not my will, but thine be done."

There is a story James Boyce relates of an effect that happened in Donald Grey Barnhouse's ministry. One early morning early in Barnhouse's ministry, as he was still a minister very young in his ministry experience, a woman came to him, and she said, "I have a son who is sick and dying with tuberculosis in my home. Would you come and visit?"

Barnhouse said, "Yes, of course! I will come and visit."

She said "He's an unbeliever and he's very bitter."

Barnhouse replied, "I'll come with you right away."

She said, "No, please don't come with me right away, wait. Because if you come with me, he will know I have called you and because of his bitterness he will react in anger and rage."

So Barnhouse waited an hour and went and knocked on the door. As she opened the door and let him in he greeted her, and, walking in, noticed the bed with the young man in the front room. He acknowledged the young man and introduced himself as "Donald Grey Barnhouse. I'm a minister in this neighborhood." The man immediately began to curse and to act angry towards Barnhouse saying, "Why does God allow me to spit my lungs into this cup? Why does God hate me so much as to cause so much suffering in my life? Why does he bring this upon me? What have I ever done to God?" As the rage continued to grow, Barnhouse was left with nothing but to excuse himself. And so he left and within the week the young man died.

Some years later another woman came to Barnhouse with a situation very similar. She had a son who was dying with tuberculosis and asked that Barnhouse would come and visit. Barnhouse was a little bit reluctant because he remembered what happened last time, but he knew his obligation was to go. So he told her he would come. She said, "Then come now." So he went with her to the house. He entered the house and found a very similar scene—a very ill man and a bed in the front room. He walked up to the man, introduced himself, and the man said, "Yes, I recognize you. I know you."

He heard at that point this young man's testimony of his love for Christ. He told Barnhouse that over the past years he had really only had enough strength to get up from his bed about one hour out of 24. He used that hour to walk around the block of his neighborhood. One time as he was walking around the block of his neighborhood, he passed the theater. As he approached the theater, which had lights on, he decided to go in and rest because he was fatigued. When he went inside and sat down, he found Dr. Barnhouse in there preaching, as they were having a meeting—very typical in Philadelphia in those days when revival meetings would take place in theaters and in public areas.

As Barnhouse was preaching the gospel of Jesus Christ, this man heard and came to love the Lord and surrendered his life to him. From that point, on his daily walks, he began to visit people in his neighborhood and talk to them about the love of Christ and his love for Christ. Others came to accept Jesus Christ as their Savior. As he lay there in the bed he asked Dr. Barnhouse if he would come and visit him the next week. Dr. Barnhouse agreed. Then he said, "I want my relatives to be here when you come to visit and I want you to speak to them."

Barnhouse agreed and when he came to that young man's house again, every room was filled. People were sitting on the steps, the kitchen was filled, the den was filled, the young man's room was filled. People were in the hallways. All of the relatives of this young man were there and Dr. Donald Grey Barnhouse spoke to them the gospel of Jesus Christ. This man gave to them his testimony. As he lay on his very own deathbed, he talked about the love of God to him and of his only hope, which was in Jesus Christ, and that there was no hope except Jesus Christ. This young man was in the Kidron Valley, was in his own Garden of Gethsemane, his body was wracked with pain and anger as he chocked and gagged with tuberculosis. And yet with every breath he spoke, he spoke nothing but of the love and the glory of God who had saved his soul.

Several weeks later, that young man also died. Now I would ask you, "What do you believe is the testimony that remains with the people who heard the gospel message and the gospel lived in the life of a man who was dying with tuberculosis?" Now let me ask you to reflect for a moment on your own circumstances in life. Believer and unbeliever will face like situations and circumstances in life. We will be frustrated by those around us, we will face sickness, we will face persecution, we will face hardship, we will face rebellious children, we will face spousal disagreements, we will face the death of our parents, we will face our own demise, we will face loss of job, we will face lose of income, we will at different points of our life be disappointed and hurt in different ways—believer and unbeliever alike. The difference is in the response of each one.

The unbeliever will be depressed and downtrodden. The one who is far from the Lord will be dragging himself through the dirt. He will not find joy, he will not find happiness, and there will be no glory to God in the difficult circumstances they face. There will only be murderous thoughts and vindictive language. There will only be hate-filled speech and plotting against circumstances. There will be anger and disappointment. For the one who knows the Lord, even difficult times are an opportunity to give thanks to God and to glorify the Lord.

Each will have a different response. What is yours? What has been yours? What would those around you say is your response to your disappointments in life? Do you "Count it all joy, my brothers, when you meet trials of various kinds?" Do you "know that the testing of your faith produces steadfastness?" "And let steadfastness have its full effect, that you may be perfect and complete, lacking in nothing." So says James. Thank God for the gift of men and women who have captured our theology in song, like those we can draw our confidence from in difficult times and trials.

The hymn "Go to Dark Gethsemane" makes this point very well.

> "Go to dark Gethsemane, You will feel the tempter's power.
> Your redeemer's conflict see, watch with him one bitter hour.
> Turn not from his griefs away, learn of Jesus Christ to pray."

This hymn writer captured the essence of where we begin the Passion of Christ. Our Lord went into the Kidron Valley and we will go with him. We will not stand at the gate to guard; we will not fall asleep while he prays. We will journey with him and we will see his suffering. And in seeing his suffering, we will come to understand, in that bitter time of suffering, not to turn away from grief, but to learn from him how to pray and how to come to the Father, and ultimately how to glorify God and count it all joy when we meet trials of various kinds.

2

Judas the "Friend" of Jesus

John 18:1–3

> When Jesus had spoken these words, he went out with his disciples across the Kidron Valley, where there was a garden, which he and his disciples entered. Now Judas, who betrayed him, also knew the place, for Jesus often met there with his disciples. So Judas, having procured a band of soldiers and some officers from the chief priests and the Pharisees, went there with lanterns and torches and weapons.

If I had my druthers, I would not take up Judas in my preaching. Why not? Well, certainly it was a dark day when Judas betrayed Christ. It was a dark day when he led soldiers to the garden to arrest Christ, to betray him with a kiss. But beyond that in exploring Judas, do we not see too much of ourselves? Not that we are lost as certainly one who would betray Christ to the cross must be. Not that we are like the one about whom Jesus said it would be better for him if he had never been born. But because we still labor under the curse of sin, aren't we also dual-minded? Isn't there too much of the first Adam that still resides in us?

So when we study Judas, can't we see shadows of Judas in our own life during times of unfaithfulness to Christ? Thus trying to examine this person Judas can be painful if we deal with Judas honestly. So I would ask that you would consider Judas, not simply as a time of regret because of this man in history who betrayed Christ—what a tragedy we have here—but because Judas represents for us such a contrast of faithfulness, truthfulness, fidelity. He is, beyond the Pharisees and the Sadducees, the definition of hypocrisy, a man who would be a friend to Christ, who would be with Christ, and yet would betray Christ for his own selfish ambition.

I've heard it said that every man has his Judas in his life. Every man will experience one whom he brings into his confidence, bring into his trust, who will prove untrustworthy and who be a traitor. Every person has his or her Judas; every church has its Judas. There seems to be enough of Judas in the context of anybody's life to go around. In every business place, isn't there a trusted co-worker or a trusted friend who will turn out not to be so trustworthy in the end. I'm convinced that, again, every church and every religious organization of any type will have its Judas. And I'm almost as convinced every man has the potential to be a Judas; every one of us has a potential to be a betrayer.

There was a radio broadcaster in 1939 who once said this about Russia, but we can apply it to Judas; "It is a riddle wrapped in a mystery inside an enigma." We puzzle when we look at Judas. We puzzle because we see a man who had three and a half years of life with Jesus and yet look how Judas' life ended. In Matthew 26 Jesus said, "It would have been better for that man if he had not been born." How could it be that it would be better for a man if he had never even been born? So heinous, so great is the crime of betraying Christ that it is better to have never lived.

Judas Iscariot—what could we say about his life except what we can observe in flotsam? Flotsam is the debris that floats in water after a shipwreck. In other words, Judas has a story, but it's nearly impossible to discover, it's nearly impossible to discern. Where did he meet Jesus? What family did he have? Where did he come from as far as his family goes? What did they think of his being a disciple? When was he away that his thinking had moved away from Christ? Did he actually ever truly grasp that his own thinking had moved so far from Christ or was his hypocrisy so complete that he had even fooled himself, even as he worked *against* Christ, that he was working *for* Christ?

We find the Scriptures give us an indication that this can be so even in our own lives. We're told there will be those who come to persecute you, and in persecuting you think they are serving God. It's possible for hypocrisy to run so deep in a man's heart that he actually believes he's at the zenith of godliness when he is working antithetical to the purposes of God. Wreckage can come from a great ship like the *Titanic*. A ship that had a great future, a long future ahead of it, one that was to be prosperous, a ship whose purpose was to be unsinkable and luxurious, and yet a ship that was wrecked on its maiden voyage, forever lost with nothing but flotsam to show, the debris that floats on the surface.

Judas had a remarkable start with Christ. He had ability, he had intelligence. We wonder what might have been, but when he arose from the Passover meal, he took another course. We wonder what might have been of one who seemed to have such promise. Whatever else his life was or may have been, he's known now only as a betrayer. Isn't that one of the tragic ironies of sin? No matter how you live your life, no matter what you do, no matter your degrees, no matter your accomplishments, no matter, if you're military, what rank you may have acquired or attained to, it doesn't really matter when you consider your legacy if there is one crime that overshadows all else.

The life of Benedict Arnold is such a one. Benedict Arnold—if we were to take the time, I could give you an impressive résumé of a well-respected man and leader, key at WestPoint, but a man who at the wrong moment made the wrong decision and cast his lot with those who would seek to keep America from becoming a nation. He thought it was the right choice. And how do we know him now? As a traitor—that's all we know about Benedict Arnold. And we even use his name when we want to describe a betrayer. So complete is the recasting of a whole and entire life that he is only a betrayer. That's all he is. And we call people *Benedict Arnold*.

So it is with Judas. Does it matter his education, his background? Does it matter what he had done, what he had learned? His achievements—we don't know them. He's simply *the betrayer*. That's all his legacy is. Take a moment, jot down a note, and ask yourself, *What will be my legacy? What will I be remembered for?* We remember ourselves one way; the story after we pass may be much different.

As the only Judean in the band of 12 disciples, Judas was respected. He came from the same royal tribe as Jesus. He was a pureblooded Jew who viewed Galileans with contempt, as many were of mixed bloodlines. Hence the saying, "Can anything good come out of Nazareth?" No, Judas among those twelve was a cut above in his bloodline. His credentials were never questioned, his loyalty was assumed. Did anyone ever question whether Judas was onboard or not? Did they ever ask Jesus, "Have you taken a good hard look at Judas?" Did they ever take a look at his résumé? His loyalty was assumed. He was trusted. He was trusted so well they gave him charge over the money.

He had proved himself in ministry as well. The disciples had gone out in a group of 70, but they had also gone out 2 by 2. There is no report of his failure or even any struggling in that ministry as he went out 2 by 2 to conduct ministry. He had preached the coming of the kingdom in Christ's name, and it had been received. He was the only one with an official title in the band. He was the *Financial Officer,* the only one with an office. He had a business mind. He received the gifts and he dispersed any benevolences.

In John 12:5, Judas shows he has a good mind for financial stewardship as well because it is there he scolds Jesus, suggesting the money has been wasted on perfume and oil when it should have been used to help the poor. It's probably the first clear indication we have that something is going on with Judas. He's still in the band of the 12, and yet now he turns to Jesus and says, "You know, I think that's unwise. And you should do this a different way." Was it Judas' intent to accuse Jesus? At this point we simply see where his thinking and his mind is not with Christ.

On the very night of the betrayal, Judas would sit in the midst of the disciples as one of them. There is no indication that anyone had any idea something was wrong with Judas. In fact, when Jesus announces there will be one who will betray him, they all begin to question themselves—I would imagine all but one. They began to ask, "Will it be me? Will it be me?" They began to proclaim, "Surely it will not be I!" Peter even, in the way Peter does, even stands up and begins to make proclamations about just how far he'll go before he will betray Jesus. He would never betray Jesus, even at the cost of his own life. It's not enough for him to say, "I don't think it's me." Peter has to give an entire exhortation and speech about how it's not going to be him, but Judas doesn't speak.

Nobody questions. They just assume, as I must assume, that Judas simply had a very self-secure look upon his face, that it would never be him. He sat there, deceiving all of them except for the Lord Jesus, who sees the hearts of all men and said, "The one who dips his bread with me will be the one who betrays me." Judas dipped his bread. How could he keep from choking on his own bread? How could he keep from choking on the bread when Jesus had said the one who dips with me will be the one who betrays me? So complete is the deception of hypocrisy in one's own mind, they can actually do those things that demonstrate their ungodliness and not see them for what they are.

How is it everyone can see our sin but us? How is it everyone else can inform us where we need to straighten up, but we will be the one voice of dissent, the only one who doesn't agree? And still we trudge right on ahead. Judas dips his bread; he eats his bread and betrays Christ.

In relating the lesson to the contemporary church, John Phillips, who was a teacher at Moody Broadcasting Network with a radio ministry there, wrote in his book, *Exploring People of the New Testament*, the following words:

> It is all too easy to deceive the saints, to go through all the motions of being a believer. And it is particularly easy to playact the part of a believer if one has been raised in a Christian home and taken from the earliest days to church and Sunday school. It's easy enough them to speak well the language of Canaan. It is easy to come and go in a local fellowship of believers and be accepted as a believer, and all the time have a heart as black as pitch and a conscience seared with a hot iron.[1]

The heart addressed Jesus as "Rabbi" but never as "Lord," that black heart of Judas'. He called Jesus "Rabbi," but search your Scripture, he never called him "Lord." He calls him "Teacher, good teacher," but never did he address him as "Lord." Love for the Savior never triumphed over despising him. I would suggest Judas despised the Lord all along, even though he never realized it. Judas heard the teaching, he saw the water turn to wine. For three and a half years he would see lepers cured, the lame begin to walk, the blind to see, the deaf would hear; nature would even prove it was subject to the power of Christ, and yet he would not love the Lord.

Jesus warned him on several occasions, such as in John 6:70, when he said, "Did I not choose you, the Twelve? And yet one of you is a devil." I imagine Judas at that point would look around and think, *I wonder who he's talking about? I wonder who it could be!* That's the nature of self-deception. That's the nature of a heart that is so dark we can't even see in it ourselves. And so he couldn't hear the warning that was given to him. Jesus warned him at the table before Judas dipped the bread and in the garden tenderly when he said, "Friend, why have you come?" *Friend, why have you come?*

Judas would go through the motions of a faithful disciple, deceiving himself until he would betray the Lord with a kiss. But our Lord knows the hearts of all men and is not impressed with hypocrisy, no matter how well it is carried out, no matter how rehearsed it is, no matter how close

---

1. Phillips, *Exploring People of the New Testament*, 140.

we are to looking like a genuine believer. Hypocrisy will never impress the Lord. Judas shows us the true hypocrisy of being. When I say *being*, I mean of hypocrisy that has consumed the whole of a person. The hypocrite's crime is that he bares false witness against himself. Hypocrisy is the vice of all vices.

Did Judas think he could pocket the silver and Jesus would just escape as he had before? Maybe, maybe because he had saw Jesus escape every time they had attempted to arrest him, he thought this would be the same and he would just come out with a profit. There is no calamity greater than lavish desire. There is no greater guilt than discontentment, and there is no greater disaster than greed. Judas would eventually be sorry and filled with remorse, but we're not told he was repentant. Sorry, filled with remorse, he could see the results of his actions and yet he was not repentant.

But Judas is only the first of a list of villains who since John 12 and the triumphal entry had been plotting to see Jesus undone. From that day when Jesus entered Jerusalem riding on a donkey, the religious leaders themselves had been plotting in their hearts to murder Jesus. They couldn't have imagined this opportunity would come from the disciples themselves. They seemed to be caught by surprise because the Passover was upon them and they had to press to get in there and arrest Jesus. Typically it was unlawful to go after and arrest people on an evening so close to the Passover, but they rushed things in. They could not hold a trial in the evening, but they went ahead and held the trial in the evening anyway.

So it seems they didn't anticipate this betrayal. This betrayal seems to have come in a moment, and they seized upon it and took advantage of it. Jewish law required that Jews remain near the city. Bethany was too far to go, and Judas would have known that Jesus would be going into the olive grove on the Mount of Olives. With the exception of the Passover meal, we have no record of Jesus residing in a home in Jerusalem. So it does seem likely that the disciples would frequently go to the garden and sleep under the sky in the open air. They'd bivouacked as it were, out in the field. It was a familiar place; it was a comfortable place for the disciples.

Maybe that helps explain why they kept falling asleep. It was a place that was familiar to them. They didn't sense a crisis. Jesus would go there often to collect himself and to pray. On this night Jesus set eight of them to stand guard. He took three with him and said, "Will you stay with me and will you pray with me?" But it was such a relaxing place, and they had been with the Lord there so often, and so they continued to doze off.

How often Judas himself had slept there as a "friend" to the Lord? Isn't that one of the ironies and one of the indictments against Judas? So faithful was the Lord in his time of prayer that Judas knew just where he could find him: "You can find them in the garden because he goes there to pray. Arrest him there because if there is one thing I know about Christ, he will be in that garden praying to the Father." The Synoptics tells us it was there Jesus often went to gather his thoughts. Judas would come to that quiet and familiar place to betray the Lord, but he wouldn't come alone.

The Jews themselves didn't have authority to execute any criminal offense or criminal prosecution against Jesus, so officers from the priests and Pharisees would come in what amounted to a small police force that would be gathered there in the temple and in the grounds of the temple. Only in the Gospel of John do Romans play such an important part. Even in the trials, the Romans play an important part.

As badly as the temple leadership had wanted Jesus, we have to wonder why they needed Judas. Have you thought about that? Why was Judas so important? Why was it they needed him to come and betray Jesus with a kiss? Some would say, "Well they couldn't recognize him in the dark?" Why wait and arrest him in the dark? There are a lot of questions here as to, "Why now? Why this place? Why Judas? Why pay 30 pieces of silver? Why not just arrest Him? Why bother paying him at all?" Some suggest there was a fear of the people, that they were concerned that Jesus had too much of a popular following and so if they arrested him in public there would be a great outcry among the people, but where were those people when they said, "Free Barabbas, Free Barabbas?"

Jesus had come in on a wave of popular support; that is true, but most of that can be accredited to the season and to what was happening there and to the recent raising of Lazarus. There was a great peak and expectation, a messianic expectation that went with the holiday. They could have ambushed Jesus on the road. They didn't have to wait and try to do it in front of a bunch of people. He could have been invited inside for a discussion and they could have arrested him inside any house or even in the courts of the temple itself. It might have had something to do with the fear of the people, but it can't *only* be a fear of the people because they could have worked this some other way. They could have followed him to the garden and arrested him.

Commentators agree that it was Jesus himself whom they feared. They feared that Jesus might—true it is that they feared he might rally his supporters, but more than that, they had seen his power. They acknowledged it. He had raised Lazarus, a fact they did not deny. They said, "We have to do something or else other people will learn of it and follow him."

Jesus had proved even to his skeptics that he possessed supernatural power, and this had been proven in miracles and in their unsuccessful attempts to arrest him in the past. They had tried to arrest him and he either outwitted them or just simply slipped away somehow and they were never able to get their hands upon him. Even one time they sent guards to arrest him and then in this twisting of their nose, the guards came back and said, "We've never heard a man speak this way before." It appeared Jesus was un-arrest-able. But now they would try again using one of his own disciples.

James Montgomery Boice concludes his comments on this with the following: "Again there is this final lesson. It concerns Judas, who was so close to Christ and yet was unsaved. I put it to you: it is possible to be quite close to Christ, to sit in a Christian church, to listen to good sermons, to hear good Bible teaching by radio, even to understand what you hear and yet fail to make a personal commitment to Christ that is the necessary human response to God's work of salvation. How foolish to come that close and yet be lost! How much wiser, by contrast, to put your faith in that One who is all-together lovely and who willingly died for your salvation!"[2]

There are many who fellowship in the body of Christ, there are many who gather in churches and all places all across our land, there are many who eat at the Lord's Table, and take of the Lord's Supper, and fellowship with one another at fellowship meals, and yet they simply don't understand. But in their pride, they trumpet that they do. They seek to prove that they do by taking up the mantle of leadership or teaching. They seek to prove not only to themselves, but others. But yet the hypocrisy will begin to emerge. The darkness of the heart will begin to emerge as the Judas within them begins to come out.

2. Boice, *The Gospel of John*, 1376.

Like Judas, they look around the table, they disdain the Lord's direction, and they rationalize their betrayal that takes the form of self-assertion against the will of the Lord. Like Judas, they look and say, "Why did you spend so much on that perfume? Why did you do so much, Jesus?" In the modern context they would say, "But why would the Lord have us to do this or to waste our expenses in this way or to do this particular ministry to those kinds of people?" Because they just think it's simply not wise. Not only do they know better than their peers, but not discerning the true nature of the Church, they know better than Christ, at least in their own minds what it is the Church should do.

Do church splits come because Christ is double minded? Do church splits come because Jesus isn't clear in his Scriptures about what his will is or that he somehow is reserved in expressing them? No, they come because Christ is locked out of many minds among the people of God.

While Judas walked with Christ, he listened to Christ, he fellowshipped with Christ, and he served Christ along with the disciples, but he never knew Christ. Believing he knew better than Christ, he betrayed Christ to the world that did see Christ and hated him. Isn't it ironic that the world is able to see Christ and to be public about their hatred of Christ, whereas the ones who are so absorbed in self-hypocrisy can't see Christ, but believe that they do?

So we would say, "Come to Christ, receive his salvation so the old man, that one who is the betrayer will die and a new one will be born." Judas was no true friend, but was an enemy from the start. His heart was set on himself and he desired that Christ would serve *his* needs according to *his* vision. There is a Friend who sticks closer than a brother, One who has served the Father and met us in our need, One who gave his life when there were none to even know why, and he is speaking to us today. We hear his voice.

3

Arrested!

John 18:3–11

> So Judas, having procured a band of soldiers and some officers from the chief priests and the Pharisees, went there with lanterns and torches and weapons. Then Jesus, knowing all that would happen to him, came forward and said to them, "Whom do you seek?" They answered him, "Jesus of Nazareth." Jesus said to them, "I am he." Judas, who betrayed him, was standing with them. When Jesus said to them, "I am he," they drew back and fell to the ground. So he asked them again, 'Whom do you seek?' And they said, 'Jesus of Nazareth.' Jesus answered, "I told you that I am he. So, if you seek me, let these men go." This was to fulfill the word that he had spoken: "Of those whom you gave me I have lost not one." Then Simon Peter, having a sword, drew it and struck the high priest's servant and cut off his right ear. (The servant's name was Malchus.) So Jesus said to Peter, 'Put your sword into its sheath; shall I not drink the cup that the Father has given me?"

What are we to make of this? What are we to make of the King of glory who was about to be rough handled by his captors, those who would come to arrest him? All the way Jesus had paced his ministry perfectly. But now a band of soldiers and police and religious professionals had arrived to arrest him and drag him away. What are we to make of this?

H. G. Wells—no great evangelist, by the way— is reported to have compared the world to a stage, on which a play has been produced and managed by God. When the curtain rose, everything was perfect, and the play progressed as planned. But then the leading man stepped on the leading lady's gown, causing her to trip and knock over a lamb and push a table into the wall, which then in turn knocked over the scenery, bringing everything down on the head of the actors. Meanwhile, behind the scenes, Wells described the director, God, as desperately running back and forth, pulling on ropes, shouting directions, and trying restore his chaotic play to its intended order.

Is that the picture of God that is presented here in the garden? H. G. Wells didn't imagine the God of the Bible. H. G. Wells pictured a little God, who despite his best intentions just struggles to pull off his plan. Some may see the night of Jesus' arrest like this. As if for just a period of time, God takes his hand off the wheel. Just for a period of time, God steps back and lets history run its course. And Jesus is in the midst of it being swept along with permission from God by history, a time when he surrendered to the power and the passion of man.

The account of the arrest in John's gospel is much different from that, however. We're not given a picture of a God who has somehow either lost or given up control. When the arresting party arrived, they were led by Judas who knew the location well. My sense is that the 30 pieces of silver were for the very service of getting them as near to Jesus as they possibly could be. Scripture is actually silent about motivation or investment of the 30 pieces. It is simply in fulfillment of prophecy that Judas was given 30 pieces of silver.

But Judas seems to be shocked and surprised later on that things have turned and gone as they did with Jesus. Now we know Judas was a willful man, and I'm no apologist for the innocence of Judas by any stretch of the imagination, but how can we imagine that this played out where Judas would now be leading, without any conviction of conscience, this band to arrest the Savior, the Messiah? Perhaps it was that the religious leadership, who had decided that Jesus would have to die, wanted to avoid spurring the people to follow Jesus, which would result in Rome coming down and removing them from power.

And so imagine them wringing their hands, wondering how they can get to Jesus. They had tried to arrest him on several occasions, but could not get their hands on him. And now he as raising people from the dead, and he was performing miracles. He had been received as he came through the gate on Palm Sunday. And so there was a great deal of energy around Him, and yet they wanted Him so desperately.

In comes Judas, and Judas has an idea. He has a plan, and he says to them, "What you want is to compare your ideas, that is, to challenge Jesus, and I'm confident Jesus will be found to be true. The only problem is Jesus won't submit to this sort of inquiry or this sort of trial. So I'll tell you what. I'll take you to him, and you can bring him here, and then force the issue, and then Jesus will then defend himself, and we will see where truth resides."

Now can we know exactly what happened? Can we know that Judas even imagined that Jesus would be in the end exonerated and proven to be true? I can't find anything in Scripture where it looks as if Judas would have believed otherwise. In fact, he had so much despair afterwards as he reflected on how things had gone that he even committed suicide. I think it's perfectly understandable to see how they might give him 30 pieces of silver because Judas might have said, "I'm not going to send you out there; I'll take you to him myself. However, it will cost because all of that goes into the coffers for the sake of the gospel, of course." And so he takes the 30 pieces of silver.

And Jesus in the garden of Gethsemane, we've already learned, posted eight to guard at the gate, and he had three with him in prayer. We might consider them a rear guard if you're military minded. But he had eight at the front watching although it was late and they were sleeping. And so Judas led his party, his band, a number of soldiers there at night, most likely expecting that Jesus and the disciples, unsuspecting, will be asleep. So they crept with torches and lanterns and clubs and swords. They crept up to the garden, and there they encountered the first eight. However, with Judas in the lead, he would be recognized, and thus would not have created suspicion. Maybe Judas called. We have no idea. We're not told. But in any event, he was able to get close enough to them to be able to approach Jesus.

We're told in the Synoptics that he even gave him a kiss. And all parties were gathered there close together, so close that when Peter pulled his sword and lunged, probably to try to behead Malchus, Malchus ducked. And so Peter only took an ear. How did they get so close except that the deceiver's deception was so complete? He was able to usher and escort them right to the very place where Jesus was with the disciples.

I'm sure the Pharisees and Sadducees knew where the Kidron Valley was. That is where David had to run from Absalom. It was legendary. I'm sure they knew of that big olive grove over there, called Gethsemane. These people were native to the land. They knew the place. So why Judas? Why the 30 pieces of silver except to get them in close to avoid a long and protracted conflict and a fight. So Judas took them all the way to Jesus.

Perhaps that is how it went. Perhaps not. But in any event, we find them there at the garden.

While the Synoptics only mention the Jews of the arresting party, John makes a point of describing the full party, a detachment of Roman soldiers that have come from the Jewish Temple with those police or guard from the Jewish Temple. While it's doubtful that a full cohort of a thousand would have come, soldiers would have been necessary because it was during the festival time in Jerusalem. In those festival times, there was an explosive atmosphere that sometimes could result in revolt. Thus it was very frequent that they would re-garrison, or reinforce the garrison that was there in Jerusalem just in case so they could keep down the possibility of revolt.

So here is the picture that we have: Romans, Gentiles, Jews, and religious leaders, police, that is the Temple guard, all coming to arrest Jesus with torches and swords, to arrest the One who is the Light of the world himself and the Prince of Peace. They bring torches to arrest the Light. They bring swords against the Prince of Peace. The picture presented by John is clear. The entire world, Jew and Gentile, have come out against Jesus, and the responsibility rests with them all.

It's fashionable to say it was the Jews who crucified Jesus. Or it's fashionable to say, "No, it was the Gentiles who crucified Jesus." It was Jew and Gentile who cooperated to arrest and crucify the Lord. The picture John presents is one where Jesus is not out of control, however. He is firmly in control. In another place, we might have felt the same when we read of a storm brewing, and the disciples in the boat, and Jesus was there asleep. As the storm came and chaos surrounded the boat, we might have felt the same threat the disciples did. And then they woke Jesus. Jesus came forward and commanded peace. He brings order into chaos.

Was there ever really any chaos? Would the Lord have slept through his own death or the perishing of the disciples? Certainly not. He commanded peace, and the storm and the waters were still. Did he take charge of the storm and the waters? He *always* had charge of the storm and the waters.

Now Jesus sat in the quiet of the garden while just like a storm cloud, a crowd approached through the darkness with torches flashing light in the dark sky just as lightning in the time of a storm. Again, chaos was approaching. Again, it came with weapons just like lightning which could take lives and threaten the lives of the apostles at the very least. But Jesus was not surprised. From the beginning, he knew that this would come to pass, and he was in charge of the situation.

Jesus had already delayed in the garden, hadn't he? Why do we say he delayed in the garden waiting for Judas to arrive? Knowing all that was to transpire, couldn't Jesus have simply left? Couldn't he have avoided the whole incident? If he couldn't have stopped them from coming, did he have to be there when they came? He had already said, acknowledging what was to come to pass, "Father, if it is possible, allow this cup to pass from me." Jesus knew the hour had come. He was in despair, and he was in great stress and turmoil over it. He knew that this was the time, and yet he lingered in the garden, waiting for his captors to arrive.

We know that he stayed until the betrayer arrived, and when they did arrive, they didn't wait for a search. They didn't go looking because Jesus walked out to greet them. He didn't wait for a command. He didn't wait for them to call. Instead, he is the One who asked them whom they are coming for. They aren't out there saying, "Has anybody seen this Jesus of Nazareth?" They weren't going through lifting covers and pulling back cloaks and looking for him. Jesus is the One who asked them, "What are you doing here? Whom have you come for?" When they said that they had come for him, he identified himself quickly.

Isn't it interesting that when they sought to make Jesus a King he fled, but when they come seeking his death he walked out to them? Whether it was a lack of light or their own inability to recognize him, they responded, "We're looking for Jesus of Nazareth. We're looking for Jesus of Nazareth."

"For whom are you looking?" We can reflect on one lesson in spiritual blindness here, can't we? Here was Jesus standing right before them. They had come to arrest him, and still when he says, "Who are you looking for?" instead of saying, "We're looking for you," they say, "We're looking for Jesus of Nazareth." They had come to arrest the Man standing plainly before them. Maybe they were distracted with the disciples. Maybe the lights or the shadows were just such that they couldn't see him. Maybe they were caught up in the process, trying to integrate a Jewish group of Temple guard along with Roman soldiers. Maybe the issues of command and control were at play. Whatever it was, Jesus had to identify himself to them.

Jesus was identified by their guide Judas when he came to kiss him, and still they were bewildered and not sure who he was. Twice, Jesus called them out. Finally, he focused their attention upon himself. Finally, they saw him for who he truly is. Jesus answered them, "I am." Romans 1 tells us that the things of this earth testify that there is a God, and that they are plainly seen by all. And that the things about God are not hidden, but they are clear, and they are evident to all who have eyes to see, that all mankind is able through natural revelation to know that there is a God. Yet we find those who would still deny that there is a God.

Just as Jesus who stood right before them said, "It is I whom you are looking for," and still they were bewildered, so creation cries out, "There is a God in heaven." And still people say, "But where is he? Where is this One who made all of this?" The Church calls and calls and calls to them, but they are so busy proving that air is invisible that they cannot hear the voice of God. Even though it echoes in their ears, they cannot hear him until suddenly God will make himself known.

It's at this point that Jesus showed them who he is. He said, "I am he. I am he." Doesn't this take us all the way back to John, chapter 1, where we learned that Jesus was the Light who had come into the world, and the Light had made himself known to his people, and his own people did not know him? They didn't recognize him for who he was. He came and he manifested himself to them, and they could not recognize the One whom they had been waiting for throughout all of Israel's history. And when God finally gave to them the One they were waiting for, they couldn't recognize him.

Isn't this the same issue playing out here? As Prophet, Jesus stepped into the light, and he revealed himself. We see here in this arrest scene the three offices of our Lord—Prophet, and Priest, and King. Here Jesus exercised the office of Prophet as he came forward and he said, "I am he." Now there is some ambiguity in the way that this can be phrased, but it is clear that the phrase *ego eimi* is the I am. That is, the identifying name of God is purposefully used by Jesus just as when he used it in his earlier discussion when he said, "Before Abraham was, I am." In that same sense, Judas, at least, would have heard and remembered the *I am* statement.

When Jesus said, "I am," they fell back. Now this is an area of confusion for many people. Some argue that the party being unexpectedly confronted by Jesus fell back in a sudden moment of guilty conscience because they had heard his teaching. They knew he was innocent. When he stepped forward with confidence, and began asking the questions, they suddenly shirked back, losing their sense of confidence in numbers.

Feeling more like individuals, they shrank back from Jesus. They heard him, and they began to fall back. Maybe Judas was the one who had a visceral reaction. It may be Judas heard the "I am he," and maybe Judas was the one in the lead. Maybe Judas fell back, and so they, not knowing what to expect, begin to back up a little bit to get a little space.

While I can understand that explanation that some would instinctively take a step back, I don't believe that is the best explanation. While they ought to have been struck with their guilt for coming to arrest an innocent man, it seems clear that John intends us to know that Jesus was letting them hear once again that he is *I am*. We see them compelled to bow at the name *I am*. Isn't that what Scripture teaches? That at the name, every knee shall bow. Don't we catch a glimpse of it here? "I am he." And they all fall before him.

As King, Jesus shows his power and authority over his enemies. Here they are with clubs, swords, and torches. And who is bowing before whom? Jesus introduces himself as a prophet. As King, they bow before him.

When Manoah in Judges 13 discovered he had been with the angel of the Lord, he fell on his face, "We shall surely die." When Balaam in Numbers 22 came before the Lord, the Lord opened his eyes, and he saw that it was the angel of the Lord standing in front of him with his drawn sword, and he fell down on his face before the Lord.

The same in Daniel 10:10. We find there he is on his hands and his knees. In Revelation 1:17, John himself, when he saw the Lord, fell at his feet as though dead. In Isaiah 40 through 55, God expresses his own Person with these words, "I am." Just as they were dumbfounded when Jesus taught in the Temple, they now staggered as they heard the overtones of God's self-disclosure from Isaiah. Ironically, their response of falling down before Jesus was more proper and right than even they knew.

John Calvin sees this as further evidence of our Lord's command of the events. He says, "The evangelist states more clearly with what readiness Christ went forth to death, but at the same time describes the great power which he exercised by a single word in order to inform us that wicked men had no power over him except so far as he gave permission."[1]

---

1. Calvin, *Commentary on the Gospel of John*, 161.

Frederic Godet, the great French commentator, is convinced that none would have heard the words like Judas who would have heard them as a threat from heaven. Judas would have known that they were a threat from heaven, and that the rest were reacting after Judas who was standing near Christ, having betrayed him with a kiss. Whichever the case, the group was thrown into confusion by these words which manifested the truth of who Jesus is, and makes us all the more confident that Jesus, just as when he calmed the wind and waves, was still in control.

Far from Jesus being swept along by the will of those who hated him, Jesus arrested the progress of them. Here we're reminded of the words of Jesus himself in John 10, when he said, "I lay down my life that I may take it up again. No one takes it from me, but I lay it down of my own accord. I have authority to lay it down, and I have authority to take it up again." It was Jesus who long before this had said, "I will be the One who gives my life. No one will take it from me." And that same sovereign power directed them to arrest only him and not the disciples.

Now we catch a glimpse of Jesus acting as a high Priest. Luther believed that this act in the garden was the greatest miracle of Gethsemane. He asked them twice whom they were looking for, and their focus went from the group and the mass to just Jesus. Why is this such a big deal? Why is it a big deal that Jesus alone was arrested? We know what they intended because we learn in Mark's Gospel that Mark had thrown on a cloak and that they tried to grab him; he had to run out of his cloak and ran toward Jerusalem naked as a result. So they would have put their hands on the disciples, but Jesus keept calling them back to himself. "Whom are you looking for?"

We might have seen them looking around at the disciples, getting ready to make arrest. Jesus draws their attention again, "Who is it that you're here for?"

"Jesus of Nazareth."

"Then stay on task, and stay with me." Again they start to look around. "Who is it that you're here for?"

"Jesus of Nazareth."

"Then I'm the One you're looking for. Let the rest of these go."

That sovereign power directing them is the same sovereign power exercised by our high Priest. It's a big deal because we are held by that same preserving grace of Christ who says to death, "I'm the One you're here for. They will go free." Our high Priest has enabled us to escape.

Hebrews 7:25: "He is able to save to the uttermost those who draw near to God through him, since he always lives to make intercession for them."

Jesus keeps us, and He keeps us safe. Second Timothy 1:12, "I know whom I have believed, and I am convinced that he is able to guard until that day what has been entrusted to me." Also Jude 24: "Now to him who is able to keep you from stumbling and to present you blameless before the presence of his glory with great joy." Putting all these things together, we're given a picture of our Lord's preserving grace such as is described in Psalm 23: "Even though I walk through the valley of the shadow of death, I will fear no evil—your rod and your staff, they comfort me."

One additional incident that we need to consider from this passage is of Peter as he attacks the servant Malchus. When Peter began to understand what was happening, he drew his own weapon and struck the head of the first one he could reach. Most likely, he was emboldened at seeing them fall back, emboldened to pull out his sword and press the attack against the ones who were falling back, rather than let them regroup.

Strategically, I can't really fault his decision. If you're outnumbered, and you have a larger and better armed group, and that group falters and falls back, you need to press that attack. You need to press it on before they can regroup and come after you again with a larger force. Peter instinctively did that to protect his Lord, Jesus, whom he loves, just as he has said he would do.

He drew out a sword. He swung at the servant. Do you think that he swung simply to remove an ear? This was an act meant to take the life of a servant. You don't pull out a knife and stab at someone's head unless you intend to do some damage. The servant ducked, and Peter only got his ear.

Luke the physician is careful to point out to us that Jesus then touched and healed that ear. John just tells us that Jesus rebuked Peter and reminded him that the cup that was set before him was his to drink. How profound is that statement? He prayed just a little earlier in the garden, "Father, if it's at all possible, remove this cup from me." But now he tells Peter, "There is a cup that my Father has set before me, and it's my duty to drink it. And I will drink that cup."

We can appreciate Peter's zeal, but how true are Paul's words in Romans 10:2 that a man can have a zeal for God but without knowledge. The devastating effect of Peter's lack of genuine understanding will be seen in the hours that follow because his courage will melt away as he denies Christ.

Two cups are before us in Scripture. Psalm 116:13: "I will lift up the cup of salvation and call on the name of the LORD." Isn't this the cup we reflect on when we come to the Lord's Table? The other is the cup of God's wrath so often spoke about. That is the cup Jesus prayed might pass, and the cup he now insists on taking.

Every person will drink from one of these cups—every single person. In fact, we might say that those who are in Christ also have drunk from the cup of wrath as we have died in Christ. However, it's Christ who drank the cup, and we only as we are found in him. Truthfully, those in Christ have drunk both from the cup of wrath and from the cup of salvation. But there is only the cup of wrath for those who are not in Christ.

There was no power on earth that could interrupt the plan of redemption that was being accomplished in Christ, so we're left only with these three questions. *Have you heard Jesus calling you from the darkness?* As you have approached, have you heard him calling, and do you recognize that voice?

Secondly, *have you recognized his lordship?* Have you bowed a knee to the King of kings, or do you stand stubbornly saying, "I bow to no one"? And then finally, *has Jesus himself stepped between you, and has he taken the cup of God's wrath and drunk it all down for you that the wrath of God would be expended, and that we would only die as we die in him to be raised again in him?*

These are the questions that haunt us from the arrest of Jesus, not an issue as H. G. Wells said of God's being out of control. That is a terribly immature and purely literary approach to this text. What we're faced with is the love of Christ who stepped forth to protect his people, who had an unwavering commitment to go to the Cross, to take the cup of God's wrath for his people—of Christ who never, ever was out of control, and never ever lost a single one whom God had given him—ever to this very day.

4

The Inquisition

John 18:12–14

> So the band of soldiers and their captain and the officers of the Jews arrested Jesus and bound him. First they led him to Annas, for he was the father-in-law of Caiaphas, who was high priest that year. It was Caiaphas who had advised the Jews that it would be expedient that one man should die for the people.

Beginning in these verses everything is changed in the gospel narrative, in the story line which we are following. Up to this point, Jesus had shown everyone that he was master of every circumstance. He had been free to travel wherever he wished unencumbered. He taught whatsoever inspiration led him to speak.

When confronted with verbal challenges by those who were trained in the art of religious rhetoric, he was proved to be the Master of rhetoric. When confronted by nature or the laws of physics, he proved that he was Master of wind and wave. And when confronted with the death, he proved himself to be the Master of life as he was able to heal those who were sick, as he was able to bring back from the grave those who were deceased. Even when forces of evil, the servants of Satan themselves confronted him, he mastered them in such a way that they confessed that he was the Lord, the Son of God Most High. And when it was Satan himself who came to Jesus, he also was dispatched by our Lord who was the Master of all, even of those now about to arrest and to try him.

A movement from good to evil, from virtue to vice, depends often upon a deception—a moment when it appears that something is good when it actually, because of the heart of the one who is accomplishing it, is evil. Now there is a moment when hypocrisy will seem to bridge all that has been good with the evil that follows. You will recall that the kiss of Judas, which is included in three of the Synoptics accomplished just that. That which should have been the kiss of a friend, because of the heart of the one who gave the kiss, was actually a kiss of hypocrisy. And we found in that moment a transition in our gospel account from Jesus in the garden of Gethsemane to Jesus now being arrested and carried in for trial.

Francois de La Rochefoucauld who lived in the 1800s said, "Hypocrisy is the homage that vice pays to virtue."[1]

Why would I focus so much on that? I think because I was struck profoundly by the transition in our Scriptures. Jesus, who was un-arrestable before, Jesus, who was Master of all things before—as we move through the trials we will see that everything Jesus did was in the open, and yet with the hypocrisy of a heart filled with deceit, Judas came forward as a friend. This leads to a transition to events that were completely foreign to Jesus. It seems impossible that these events could take place, and yet, here it is before us. Our Lord going to trial.

Augustine's comments sum up this moment of betrayal by the hypocrite Judas as well. He said, "After that, his persecutors had through the treason of Judas taken and bound the Lord who loved us and gave himself for us and whom the Father spared not but gave him up for us all that we may understand that there was no praise due to Judas for the usefulness of his treachery, but damnation for the willfulness of his wickedness."[2] And with that, we leave the traitor, and we leave the quietness of Gethsemane. Our Lord bound and under guard is led to the house of Annas.

Annas, was a high priest appointed in AD 7 at the age of around 87 years, and he held the position until AD 14. Since this was the first of two religious trials or inquisitions, and since this one ended without a verdict, we can look at this more as an inquisition than a trial. A formal trial would take place before the high priest Caiaphas and the entire Sanhedrin, of which Annas was a member. And yet, there is an air here of an informal, although official investigation.

Some hold that Annas was a high priest *de jour* and that Caiaphas was high priest *de facto*. In other words, there was something about Annas that people held in such high regard and high esteem that they looked to him as the real high priest even though there would be other high priests

---

1. Rochefoucauld, *Bartletts*, 264.
2. Augustine, *Nicene and Post Nicene Fathers*, 418.

appointed, again *de facto*. According to the historian Josephus, he was one of the most influential persons among the priestly cast of that time. He would have five sons who themselves would become high priests. His grandson would become high priest. And Caiaphas was his son-in-law. So we are looking at a very influential family, and here is the patriarch of that family.

One of them, Annas II, took the post in AD 62, and during his three-month tenure, he had James, who was the brother of Jesus, stoned. Thus history's perspective on the clan of this man will not be kind, however rich his life may have been in the flesh. Gleaning accounts from the New Testament, from Josephus, from rabbinical literature, German professor Josef Blinzler summarizes their legacy and reputation as a "family that was committed to intrigue, denouncing others, and making mischief." What an interesting commentary that characterizes so many even through today; we must also be careful because this shows how quickly the life of a religious individual can become one committed to intrigue, denouncing other people, and making mischief among God's people.

Gaechter, in his book *The Hatred of the House of Annas*, points out that from the crucifixion to the fall of Jerusalem in AD 70, every time persecution broke out against the Christians, someone from his family was the high priest. What a commentary this man has on his life! He himself was wealthy. His wealth most likely had come, history seems to have discovered, from the sale of sacrifices in the court of the Gentiles. You might remember that court because that was the court Jesus went into and turned over the tables where they were selling those sacrifices, declaring that they had turned the Lord's house into a den of thieves.

He was wealthy, ambitious, energetic, and a skilled diplomat. John alone includes the account of this inquisition although he leaves out the details of the trial before Caiaphas, which the Synoptics include. However, John does mention that the trial occurred, and so we are able to conclude that there were two stops, not just the one. John mentions in verse 13 that this was the first, indicating that there was a second. And then in verse 24, he says clearly that Jesus was sent bound to Caiaphas, and then he repeats the same in verse 28.

Annas was presiding over two lower courts, and some have said that that is why Jesus was taken there. Others have said his house was located along the way, and so it was a natural stop. His son-in-law Caiaphas, who was serving as high priest, would have presided over the superior court.

The Sanhedrin ordered the arrest, and since Annas was himself a member of the Sanhedrin, he would have known that Jesus could not be tried in a lower court. This leaves us with the mystery of why Jesus was stopped at the *de jour* high priest's home.

Verse 13 alludes to the reason for stopping in the house of Annas. "First they led him to Annas, for he was the father-in-law of Caiaphas, who was high priest that year." I think we find right there a substantial reason. He was the father-in-law of Caiaphas. Because it is against Jewish law to hold trials at night, no formal charges had been made against Jesus. The arrest itself was illegal. There was nothing about this that was according to custom or law. And because Judas himself was a disciple who had turned informant, they really lacked any credibility in their case. In other words, the DA needed more to go on to take this to trial.

Thus they brought Jesus for a private hearing that was more official than unofficial. Annas wanted to know how Jesus would defend himself. We can see this in verses 19–24.

> The high priest then questioned Jesus about his disciples and his teaching. Jesus answered him, "I have spoken openly to the world. I have always taught in synagogues and in the temple, where all Jews come together. I have said nothing in secret. Why do you ask me? Ask those who have heard me what I said to them; they know what I said." When he had said these things, one of the officers standing by struck Jesus with his hand, saying, "Is that how you answer the high priest?" Jesus answered him, "If what I said is wrong, bear witness about the wrong; but if what I said is right, why do you strike me?" Annas then sent him bound to Caiaphas the high priest.

No doubt Caiaphas was counting on his seasoned father-in-law to bring some material, to get from Jesus a quote or some line of reasoning that would help formalize charges against Jesus. In other words, Annas was playing a game of "gotcha" with Jesus, trying to hear from Jesus' own mouth some compromising expression that would give adequate reason for condemnation.

We know the Sanhedrin struggled with the issue of charges because the Synoptics tell us that they paraded a string of false witnesses who gave false testimony, oftentimes contradicting even themselves. They had no real witnesses against Jesus. They had no real charge against Jesus. They were hoping that in the process of trial a charge would emerge that they could grab hold of. And so Annas worked with Caiaphas to help him put together a trial. Annas questioned Jesus about his disciples and his teaching. And while Jesus' teaching and habits outwardly conformed to the generally accepted norm and the practice of rabbis, they were still quite unconventional. So Annas was seeking for detail. For one thing, Jesus was not officially a scribe or a rabbi, and it was generally known that he wasn't formally trained or commissioned to teach. So his teaching and especially his courting of disciples drew attention and suspicion.

In addition, Jesus didn't just restate or pass along what he had been taught. He didn't, in other words, simply say, "This was the reading of God's Word, and here is what it means." He spoke with prophetic authority and gave such expanded commentary as to bring clarity to many of the teachings. In other words, in the Ten Commandments, he was asked which was the greatest. And how did he summarize that? With the two—to love the Lord thy God with all thy heart, soul, and mind, and to love our neighbor as ourselves. It was this kind of teaching that was controversial in the ears of the Pharisees and the Sadducees, and yet they couldn't condemn it because it was truth. But it was unconventional. It was different. And it caused them some consternation.

Annas sought to draw out of Jesus some confession of his intention to teach beyond the accepted interpretations of the day. His question about the disciples was intended to more or less frame Jesus as fanning the flames of the messianic movement, which they had such great concern about in those days. Why ask about the disciples? They were left unmolested in Gethsemane when Jesus was arrested. Why ask such a pointed question about the disciples?

It says in verse 19, "The high priest then questioned Jesus about his disciples and his teaching." These two areas. He didn't ask about the raising of Lazarus. He didn't ask about the feeding of 5,000. He didn't touch on any of the miracles of Christ. He wanted to know officially about the teaching and officially about the disciples—those who were with Jesus. In other words, "Are you beginning a messianic uprising, and are you teaching anything contrary to the accepted interpretations of our day?" He didn't care anything about the signs that substantiated it. Circumstances had nothing to do with it. He was looking for some opportunity to bring a charge. It seems clear one of the concerns was that Jesus would begin a movement, and the disciples were that beginning.

Dutch commentator Klaas Schilder remarked, "This insinuation suggests that Jesus [was] preaching a secret doctrine to an exclusive circle, or at least that he [was] preparing plans for a surreptitious conspiracy against the existing authorities."[3] What this question presupposes is that they didn't really know what Jesus was up to. He wanted to know, "When you're with these disciples, what is it that you're telling them? Are you telling them that you're the Messiah? Are you telling them that they must rise up and overthrow the existing authorities, that we must stand up against Rome? What is it that you're teaching them in the private councils?"

Jesus responded very clearly. Even with the messianic expectations of that time, that the Messiah would come from unknown origins—in fact, some would even say that the Man who would be the Messiah might not even realize he was the Messiah until the time when God awakened within him that awareness—there was a great deal of speculation. Messianic fever was rampant in that time, and that is the environment in which Jesus was ministering.

The Messiah, they believed, would gather a closed and secret group of supporters to begin his ministry, and then would explode upon the scene and overthrow all that was existing and replace it with a messianic government. So in short, this is what Annas was asking Jesus when he asked, "Exactly who are you?" He wondered maybe if there was something beneath the surface with Jesus. If there was any way that we could give Annas any benefit of a doubt, we might say that at this point he might have been asking Jesus, "This is the time, Jesus. This is it. If you are this Messiah, then you need to explain that now because from here we're going to Caiaphas."

So was he in the same vein as Judas? Was there some deception in what seemed to be a genuine question? Jesus answered him quite clearly because he didn'tt forward any new defense. He made no defense at all. He responded that there wasn't any mysterious cult of secrets, but instead said that every question had been answered in the clear light of day. It was answered in the Temple. It was answered in the synagogue. It was answered among the masses. All his ministries and teachings had done nothing except encourage those seeds which God planted in the nation of Israel.

---

3. Schilder, *Christ on Trial*, 31.

Secret doctrines and plots to overthrow do not belong to the plans of Jesus. There were no private councils and secret meetings. That was what the high priest was involved in. That was the reputation of Annas. That was his reputation as one who was a despiser of others and sought to overthrow others. That belonged to that cast, not to Jesus. All that Jesus did was open, and clear, and transparent. No secret meetings. No secret plans. No secret teachings.

Thus Jesus asked a probing question, and one which we would do well to meditate on ourselves. He asked Annas, "Why are you examining me?" Isn't that an interesting question from one who had just been arrested and apprehended? "Why are you examining me? Why do you ask me," he said in verse 21. "Why are you asking me these things?" Jesus was implying that Annas already had the answers to the questions, but the answers were not satisfactory.

Schilder paraphrases Jesus' response and then amplifies it for clarity for us. He says, paraphrasing Jesus, "You act as though you were perplexed about what is the real state of things. And as you ask me now to lift the veil for you, you present your petition in the guise of a prayer on the part of the uninformed, but that prayer is essentially..." and listen carefully to this phrase, "... a mask covering the enmity of the unwilling."

In other words, Annas was masquerading as someone who actually had a care and concern. What he really had was a vindictive hatred, and he was unwilling to hear. He had a mask of care and concern, and he was coming to Jesus and saying—I'm sure, very politely—"Jesus, could you just explain yourself? Help me to understand your disciples. Help me to understand your teaching." Jesus uncovered this mask that was covering an enmity of unwillingness. Annas would not understand. He had no interest in understanding. He had no desire to learn. The enmity of the unwilling.

How often have you, like me, been asked questions about Christ, or about the Church, or about the Christian faith, and you find yourself explaining once again, over and over again that which you've explained before, and that which is clearly taught and has been taught in all the history of the Christian Church? We have faced interrogations and inquisitions of our own that are motivated less by a desire to know than by the enmity of the unwilling. All they want is for you to misspeak. They aren't interested in truth. They're interested in finding somewhere your

Achilles' heel where they can get you. That is all they're interested in—that moment when they can get you.

All of Jesus' ministry, all of his teaching, all he had done, even those who owed their very life because they had died to Jesus, none of that was put on the table. None of the success, none of the blessing, none of the feeding of those who were hungry, none of the healing of the sick, none of that is on the table. We're looking for that little wedge we can use to bring separation.

In Isaiah 29, Isaiah speaks of a straying people and of faithless leaders. "Astonish yourselves and be astonished; blind yourselves and be blind! Be drunk, but not with wine; stagger, but not with strong drink! For the LORD has poured out upon you a spirit of deep sleep, and has closed your eyes (the prophets), and covered your heads (the seers)." Because they shut their heart to his message and were unwilling, they are judged and struck blind and made unable.

Here is where Jesus is well contrasted with his judge. His judge had heard the doctrine taught, and was now searching for some phrase or some single word that would condemn Jesus, whereas Jesus was reminding him that he had already heard all that there was to hear. Jesus added a second dimension to his defense—if we will call it that, recognizing there was no new defense offered. He simply readdressed it with questions. He first clarified his intention. Everything was out there. Everything was open. The second was to point out its effects. Jesus said, "Ask those who have heard from me."

Jesus counted among his disciples the poor, the uneducated, and the common men, and so his mission, his doctrine, and faith in him isn't a question of mere knowledge and secret instruction, but a question of self-assertion or self-denial in obedience to God. Again, as Schilder put it, "The appropriate question is to ask not what do you know, but in what is your life rooted."[4] Do you draw your sustenance from the Spirit or from the flesh?

We can conclude this portion of the trial with a realization and a question. Realize that when Jesus suggested that Annas ask those who had heard him to testify as to the doctrine he was teaching, he was implicating us in his trial. When Jesus said, "Ask those who have heard my teaching," we were implicated in the trial for we also have heard his teaching. And

---

4. Ibid., 42

we are the ones who now will bear witness and testimony in the defense of Christ. Not that we would undo the trial, not that we would undo its effects, but we stand just as those did then in defense of the teaching of our Savior. "Ask those who have heard." We have heard, and so we also stand with them. We are implicated by Christ in his trial.

The second question: When asked, how will you answer? When asked about the teaching of Christ, how will you answer?

5

Peter's Denial

John 18:15–18, 25–27

Simon Peter followed Jesus, and so did another disciple. Since that disciple was known to the high priest, he entered with Jesus into the court of the high priest, but Peter stood outside at the door. So the other disciple, who was known to the high priest, went out and spoke to the servant girl who kept watch at the door, and brought Peter in. The servant girl at the door said to Peter, "You also are not one of this man's disciples, are you?" He said, "I am not." Now the servants and officers had made a charcoal fire, because it was cold, and they were standing and warming themselves. Peter also was with them, standing and warming himself.

Now Simon Peter was standing and warming himself. So they said to him, "You also are not one of his disciples, are you?" He denied it and said, "I am not." One of the servants of the high priest, a relative of the man whose ear Peter had cut off, asked, "Did I not see you in the garden with him?" Peter again denied it, and at once a rooster crowed.

As they left Gethsemane, the disciples scattered. Mark, we are told in another of the Synoptics, had to flee naked for they grabbed for his cloak, and tore it off his body. He escaped into the night without clothing on, so hasty was his escape. So punctuated was the panic of that night. This chapter picks up with the journey of two of those apostles, John and Peter who were following Christ from afar, hiding in the shadows and the darkness as Christ was on his way to the inquisition.

Denial versus betrayal. Judas lied. He lied, perhaps unknowingly. Perhaps he was duped. He had a different vision. Whatever his motivation, he betrayed Christ into the hands of Christ's enemies.

Peter—Peter also was lying, and he was nearby to Christ, standing afar off. He followed at a distance. Some make too much of an allegory of Peter's staying too far away, and they seek to make application that we also would stay too far away, and we need to draw unto Christ. That is a true statement. We do oftentimes stay at a distance from Christ when we ought to be drawing near to Christ, but that is not necessarily the application of why Peter followed at a distance. He followed at a distance because he was under threat of being arrested! And so he followed in the shadows. Certainly we can say Peter was not lacking courage, for we find him there in the very court nearby where Jesus was. But his crime was not betrayal; it was denial.

Judas, in the words of Tennyson, had an unfaithful faith "and faith unfaithfully kept him falsely true."[1] True to the purposes of God, and yet he was under the wrong pretense. He had an unfaithful faith because he did carry out exactly that which he was purposed to do, and yet he did so with infidelity to the person of Christ.

All four gospels tell us the sad story of Peter's denial—all four. Not only was this a stinging blow because Peter was an intimate disciple to Christ, a stinging blow to the people of God because here we have one who was a strong disciple, but one also on whom Jesus seemed to base the future of the Church when he said, "On you I will build my Church." Clearly, Jesus was separated and alone in his suffering and death because at this point, even the most faithful, even the most stalwart disciple was torn away from his side. Stripped away from those who love him, Christ was now alone in his suffering.

Structurally, John interweaves the denials and prayer to show that while Peter warmed himself and acted like a coward, Jesus stood under inquisition, denying nothing. What a contrast in the basic picture we have of the one who said, "I will die for You," and yet he drew near to a fire to warm himself, cowering in fear, and lying, and denying Christ, while Christ not far off at all was standing under the accusations of the high priest, denying nothing, being faithful and true and transparent, and also taking a step closer to the Cross.

Gethsemane had now quiet. The torch light was gone. The sound of the soldiers' footsteps had grown quiet, not even an echo to be heard. The disciples had all fled, and the Lord had been taken to Annas. Gethsemane

---

1. Tennyson, *Century Dictionary*, 4393.

stood as a silent testimony to what was. Now a sad place. A place of quiet.

Following at a distance in the darkness were Peter and another disciple who almost certainly was John. There has been debate, of course, throughout history, but there is very little evidence to support the suggestions of any other disciple. We're told that the disciple knew Christ. We're told that this disciple knew the high priest. That is probably based on 19:27, because there we can surmise that John would have had a house in Jerusalem. As a citizen of Jerusalem, he would have encountered the high priest throughout his life. In Mark 1, we also discover that John's father was at least wealthy enough—well off enough—to have a couple of servants, which would have caught this group of priests' attention anyway. And so it's quite probable that this was John, and having lived there in Jerusalem for some time, he knew that cast of the high priest and their servants.

Furthermore, a Galilean probably wouldn't have had access to the courts of the high priest. A Galilean with his accent would have been quickly identified. During the celebration of Passover, in the time of any celebration of any feast in Jerusalem, there would have been people from all over who gathered there, and those from outlying provinces would have been quickly identified. But John, whom we believe this to be, had now moved past Peter, leaving Peter in the shadows. We aren't sure exactly why Peter hung back. Perhaps he was afraid that he would be discovered. John moved forward in confidence, knowing the high priest, and gained entry into the atrium, essentially the courts of the high priest's home.

This is not the place where Jesus himself was being queried, but it's the courts outside of that place. John went in. Something made him remember that Peter was outside, and so he went back and petitioned to allow Peter to enter as well. But Peter did not continue to walk with John. John apparently moved to some corner where he was able to observe both the court—because he gives us such detail in saying that the fire even was a charcoal fire—and Peter. Also with an ear and an eye, he was able to hear what was happening with Christ. It's unlikely that he went inside the very room where the inquisition was being held, but it is likely that he was able to peek through or to see or to hear, being stationed at some wall nearby.

Peter is the one Jesus called *Cephas* in Aramaic, or *Petros* in Greek, which means *rock*. Rock is not a proper name. Rock is a very unusual word to be used for a name or to give someone. It means literally—rock. That is just what it means—rock. It's an odd name to assign to the character of a man to whom you are willing to pay a complement, and yet Jesus gave this to Peter with high praise because he said, "And on you I will build my Church."

This Church that will grow out of Jerusalem will be built upon solid rock, Peter—Peter the person? Far more likely the very confession which Peter has given. Remember, when Jesus said, "Who do the people say that I am?" it was Peter who proclaimed, "You are the Christ, the Messiah, the Son of God." Jesus turned, and said, "You've said well. This you did not figure out on your own, but the Spirit has revealed it to you—the Spirit of the Father."

It's most likely that it's on that very confession of faith that the Church will be built, that same confession of faith which week after week we profess not only in creeds, which is a form of our confession, but in everything that we do at church. Isn't our worship, isn't our church, isn't our faith built upon this very rock, that we like Peter say, "You are the Lord. You are the Messiah. You are the Son of God, the One who is sent to take away the sins of the world"? And on that rock, the Church is built.

Peter personified that. He spoke that in the presence of the disciples, and so Jesus turned, and he said, "On you I'm going to build my Church." Rock. Cephas. Petros. But that will not be his reputation based on this night, for on this night he will deny the One he has called Messiah. Jesus told Peter that he would deny him, but Peter promised, "Though all men forsake you, I will not." Peter said those words. He promised explicitly, "Though anyone else might forsake you, I absolutely will not. I will die before I forsake you." Then Jesus warned him. Satan desired to have him to sift him like wheat. But Jesus promised that he prayed for Peter that his faith wouldn't fail. He promised him that there would be a trial delivered upon his head by Satan himself because Satan desperately wanted to get his hands on one whom Christ had pointed to and said, "The future of the Church will rest upon this rock." And you know Satan desired to destroy that rock. But Jesus promised him, "Your faith won't fail, Peter. Your faith won't fail."

Still we've learned that Satan is the sifter of God's wheat. In God's providence, this often works to separate wheat from chaff in a person's life. The hardship experienced in a time of trial and tribulation produces hope and character. Just as we read in Paul's journey, when the ship was about to be sunk, when all the sailors were 14 days without food, when they were under trial and tribulation, it was then Paul called them to faith and to unity and to the work. It was then that Paul's own character was put on display for them because the fires often refine a man's and a woman's character.

Fires are what shape us and form us and cause us to be pliable in the hands of God because when things are good, we are stalwart and stubborn. But when things are bad and we're looking for relief, then we find where our faith is coming from—the world or the Lord. And if we are a people of faith, then our direction will move closer and closer to the Lord as we move away from the place that was a place of comfort.

In 1 Corinthians, chapter 5, the Scriptures teach that a man is delivered over to Satan for the destruction of his flesh by the church so that his spirit may be saved in the day of the Lord. Some would see it as a rather perverse ministry to take someone who is troubled, someone who is in sin, and to turn them over to the world, into the hands of Satan that Satan would crush their flesh. But how else will a church deal with one who is determined to continue that sin and to profane the very Body of Christ with that sin? How else will they be purified except to be placed back into the furnace that the dross can be burned away? In this way, Satan serves the purposes of God by burning the dross away. In his attempt to crush, he actually purifies.

The man's sin had brought dishonor to the Lord's name in that church. He was a professing Christian, but Paul told the church to have no fellowship with him, and the man was put back out into the world from which he came, out of the fellowship of the saints, away from the means of grace. He was put into a course of trouble and sorrow. What was the result? The result was his confession of sin and recovery as, according to 2 Corinthians 2, the sinner is restored by grace. Through his isolation, he discovered what he lacked. He was put outside of his family, and so he came back bearing the confession of a sinner seeking recovery and restoration.

Can this be God's purpose with Peter? Will Cephas be made fit for service by experiencing his own unworthiness, and upon realizing that he can only follow Christ after Christ has died for him? Peter followed after Christ, but he couldn't follow Christ to the Cross. He couldn't follow Christ to the trial. Christ had to go this route alone, and he would be left alone, and he would cry out from the cross that he was alone in his suffering and in his anguish under the wrath of God. But *only* he could do it, and if Peter were to share it with him, it would contaminate the sacrifice of our Lord by mixing that which was impure with that which was pure.

In our passage, let's first note what Peter did right. There is some redeeming grace in Peter here. In Gethsemane, remember it was Peter who wanted to press the attack when the arresting party faltered and fell back at Christ's words. But in obedience to Christ, he stopped, and the arresting party left with Christ. He was alone with John, and they followed at a distance all the way back to Annas' home, the atrium connected to the house.

Since a woman wouldn't be allowed in the actual Temple complex, John spoke to the girl at the gate and gained entry. It appears that John was in the lead, just as he was when he arrived at the empty tomb on resurrection morning. He remembered his friend Peter. He spoke again to the girl and asked for Peter to be allowed in. Her question is stated more as an expression of cynicism than it is any kind of an interrogation. She was not really in a place to be interrogating, in any event. Peter was in foreign surroundings. Peter was a minority party as a Galilean, and he was guilty of an assault in Gethsemane. He continued his journey with a denial.

From that point, we aren't sure what happened with John. Peter didn't advance as far. He moved into the court, and he saw a fire that was being kindled with charcoal, and he moved over to it. There he found the servant of Annas, and he may have considered his first denial a bit of cloak and dagger. And so we don't find much reflection on Peter at this point. Perhaps he thought it was just a way to get in. It was a minor compromise. He just wanted to get through the gate. But once any denial is accepted, it's just a question of extremes.

I think there is an important reason for us to pause here and reflect. Do you daily feel the strain and the weight of living in this world? Do you daily feel the pressure to compromise? If you do not feel the pressure to compromise daily, then I would submit with great confidence that you need to take a close look and reexamine your life. Peter denied Christ and did not even feel the weight of his denial. It was a means to an end, and the ends justify the means. He wanted to get closer to Christ, and to do so, he denied Christ. There is no place for the denial of Christ in the Christian's life—no place. A small compromise doesn't lead necessarily to something better; it leads to additional compromise because it's already established we're a compromiser. It's only a question of to what extreme. It's only a question of degrees not a question of *if*. And so every single day, you should be feeling the weight of your Christian conviction. Why? Because the world hates Christ.

Oh, it plays its own game of cloak and dagger. It dresses itself up in religion, but it calls you to infidelity to the Scriptures. It calls you to behave contrary to the law of God. It calls you to be unfaithful to the people of God, to the Church of Jesus Christ, and to the Lord himself. As long as you are a compromiser, you will not feel the weight of the world, but you ought to feel the conviction of your sin.

Peter—his state of mind at that moment, think about it. He had followed along in shock and disbelief as the events of that night stood in stark contrast with the triumphal entry they had so recently celebrated. Everything had turned on a dime. Everything had gone from victory and success and tranquility in the garden of Gethsemane to chaos. They were in a state of shock and disbelief. Their Master had been taken from them. They were under threat of their life, and Peter had actually pulled out his sword and had struck another man. He now was standing in the dark, implicated by his own attack against the servant.

In that cold darkness among his enemy, the high priest's steps had slowed. John went on in, but Peter stopped. His hope began to wane at that point, and he suddenly felt alone there in the enemy's camp. There was no chance for him to return to anything for everything had been scattered. His Lord was captured. The disciples had fled. He had no friends. He found himself gathered there at a fire with those who had arrested Jesus. And while Jesus was bound and buffeted, Peter began to warm himself by the fire. Matthew Henry wrote, "Those that warm themselves with evildoers grow cold towards good people and good things, and those that are fond of the devil's fireside are in danger of the devil's fire." [2]

Let me remind you again that this is Peter. This is Cephas, the one whom the Lord said he would build his Church on. And now Peter is at the fireside of those who would stand against Christ. It's Peter now standing in the company of Christ's enemies. Peter had always been the strongest of the disciples. He had always been the most committed. But it may have been that those very traits are what put him in danger now. How could it be that the one most committed, how could it be that the one who

---

2. Henry, *Matthew Henry's Commentary*, 916.

was always the first to step forward to serve the Lord, that those very traits could be the ones that would place him in danger? It was courageous to follow when most of the other disciples had fled, wasn't it?

Barclay says, "The tremendous thing about Peter was that his failure was a failure that could only happen to a man of superlative courage."[3] True, Peter failed, but he failed in a situation which none of the other disciples even dared to face. He failed not because he was a coward, but because he was a brave man. The circumstances Peter found himself in were because of his courage. Peter's courage showed itself in overconfidence on several occasions.

When Jesus warned the disciples that they would all flee from His side, Peter looked around the room at his peers, and then he said confidently that while he couldn't speak for what they would do, he certainly would never flee. Mark records Jesus' warning in chapter 14, and Peter says plainly there and emphatically, "If I must die with you, I will not deny you." Peter demonstrated courage by following Christ, by standing there in the place where he could be accused not only of being a disciple, but of attempted murder against one of the priest's servants, but that same courage resulted in an overconfidence, and finally denial.

Perhaps the answer is that, as Johann Peter Lange noted "an assumed boldness is a characteristic symptom of fear."[4] He assumed he would be bold. He assumed he would be fearless. He assumed he would be courageous. And yet when the test came, he failed. Proverbs 20:6: "Many a man proclaims his own steadfast love, but a faithful man who can find?"

Now let's be reminded of Jesus' prayer for Peter. He prayed that his faith would not fail. Had it? Had Jesus' prayer failed? Jesus is praying that Peter's faith would not fail, and it didn't, although his courage did. Look at the contrast in verse 18 and verse 26 where it says that Peter stood "with them," and then in 26, it says but he had been standing "with him." Now Peter stands with them. He had been standing with him, that is Jesus. When difficult times come, in whose company are you to be found? In 1 Corinthians 15:33, "Do not be deceived: Bad company ruins good morals." When difficult times come, whom will you be standing around?

After the second denial, Peter was confronted with an eye witness. Perhaps the fire flared up, perhaps there was a spark that went up. In the

---

3. Barclay, *The Gospel of John*, 269.
4. Lange, *Commentary on the Holy Scriptures*, 553.

shadows, the distinct features of Peter's face began to emerge, but one was there who knew that Peter was out there in the garden of Gethsemane. He was an eye witness. And here Peter was finally forced, not into some sort of a passive denial. He is forced to outright lie in the face of evidence against him.

A man said, "I saw you out there in the garden. I saw you. I'm not guessing you might be a disciple. I'm telling you I was there, and I saw you." And Peter swore, and he cursed, and not only did he say, "Oh, I don't know what you're talking about," but now he spoke specifically of Christ. "I don't know this Man." Like the kings of Israel, he knew his own strength was not sufficient because now he had been sifted by the devil. Now he knew he was a fake. Now he knew he was a coward. Now he knew he was a hypocrite. And when the cock crowed, it was almost a sacramental seal on Peter's denial and the truth of the Lord's prophecy. Mark notes that Peter remembered and at that point was a broken man, weeping. Spiritual poverty had come on him quickly, and he stood empty handed, alone, and with the enemies of his Lord.

So now I have to ask you—*Have you been seen in the garden with him?* Have you been with him in Bible study? Have you been with him in prayer? Have you been with him in worship? If you've been with him, have you been seen with him? When others think of you, do they see you by the fire or by the Lord? In that last question asked of Peter, we can hear the expectation of the world for someone who has truly been with the Lord.

Isn't it interesting that those who are in the world have a higher expectation of those who walk with Christ than sometimes Christ's own disciples have of themselves? The world expects that if you profess faith in Christ that you will have a life so ordered as to be like Christ. The disciples of Christ, to include ourselves, are far too easy on ourselves when it comes to walking with the Lord. If you've been with him, and you have been seen with him, isn't it fair that the world would expect you to be committed to him?

James Montgomery Boice comments, "We say we're in Christ. We say that we are Christ's own, that he is our Savior and Lord. We are seen in his company, therefore we should profess what he professes. If we do not profess that, if we do not receive his teaching personally, then he is not our Lord no matter what we may say. His priorities are our priorities, his values are our values, and we cannot borrow the culture of the world."[5]

Boice goes on to tell the story that is told by Spurgeon. And in that story, a young lady is struggling, and she is grappling with the faith. She is in the world, and yet she professes Christ. And Spurgeon tells her to go outside of the church that night and to look for the train that would take her home. And he said, "You have three choices when you come to that train. You can put a foot on the train and leave a foot on the sidewalk. And then when the train leaves, you will find yourself really in neither spot at all. You'll find yourself being drug along by the train with great injury, and you'll find yourself not getting to the destination that you intended to go to.

"Or you can stay right there on the sidewalk and not get on the train at all. And in that sense, you would be staying in the world, and you would be enjoying all the pleasures that it has because you have only your life to enjoy all that the world can give you. Or you can get all on the train, and you can travel to the destination to which that train is going."[6]

Some of us here have been sifted by Satan, and we struggle with our place in the world and with Christ. Some have shrunk back in a time of testing. Some have confessed Christ but have tried to live with one foot on and one foot off, and have lived more by the fire of the world than by the side of our Savior.

But even with his failures and denials, Peter had never forsaken by Christ. There is a great difference between one who has been sifted, struggled, and failed and an apostate, just as there is a difference between Peter and Judas—the difference between denial and betrayal. Every single one of us deny our Christ anytime we fail to live life perfectly according to the great commandment he has given us to love our God with all our heart, soul, and mind, to love our neighbor as ourselves. Each time we flounder, each time we fail, we, whether passively or actively, have denied our Lord. Each time we pull back, and we don't speak of our Lord in testimony, we have denied our Lord. Each and every time.

Are we lost? Are we like Judas? No, unless we are apostate. There was another fire that Peter would find himself beside—a fire that was kindled by our Lord Jesus Christ on which he was cooking a breakfast of fish. He

---

5. Boice, *The Gospel of John*, 1416.
6. Ibid., 1416.

called to Peter to come to that fire. And at that fire, not the enemies of Christ, but Christ himself greeted Peter. At that fire, Jesus had a conversation with Peter and reminded him of grace, and of love, and of hope, and of acceptance, and of restoration, and that he was Cephas on whom the Church will be built.

Three times Peter denied, each one progressively worse. Three times Jesus would ask him, "Do you love me?" each one progressively digging deeper into Peter's soul until Peter—with the same emotion with which he cursed and denied his Lord would finally say, "Lord, Lord, don't you know? Don't you know that I love you?" Judas knew failure. Peter knows repentance.

In conclusion of this chapter, read the words of this hymn by Helen Lemmel:

> O soul, are you weary and troubled?
> No light in the darkness you see?
> There's light for a look at the Savior,
> And life more abundant and free!
>
> Turn your eyes upon Jesus,
> Look full in His wonderful face,
> And the things of earth will grow strangely dim,
> In the light of His glory and grace.

Whatever the darkness of your night and the nature of your denial, watch for the fire provided by Jesus. Draw near to it, and hear of grace that loves you still.

6

The Jewish Trial

John 18:28–32

Then they led Jesus from the house of Caiaphas to the governor's headquarters. It was early morning. They themselves did not enter the governor's headquarters, so that they would not be defiled, but could eat the Passover. So Pilate went outside to them and said, "What accusation do you bring against this man?" They answered him, "If this man were not doing evil, we would not have delivered him over to you." Pilate said to them, "Take him yourselves and judge him by your own law." The Jews said to him, "It is not lawful for us to put anyone to death." This was to fulfill the word that Jesus had spoken to show by what kind of death he was going to die.

Have you ever wondered what the story was behind those first verses in the gospel of John, particularly in verse 11 where we look back in retrospect and wonder how the Jewish people missed it, when John tells us that the Lord came unto his own and his own did not receive him? We look back and we wonder, *"How did they miss it?"* It was all so clear. It was all there—all of the prophecies that were being fulfilled, all of the teaching that Jesus was providing, and the miracles. Certainly they couldn't deny the miracles. These scribes, and Pharisees, and these lawyers who knew the Scriptures so well, how is it that they missed it so completely?

My focus in this chapter will not be on Pilate, but rather on Jesus and the response of the Jews as Jesus is led away from the house of Caiaphas. The Jews claimed that Christ had done evil. They said he was an evil man. They also mentioned that their own law prevented them from carrying out their intentions concerning Christ.

We have already learned that Annas sent Jesus away because his interview with Jesus accomplished nothing except to keep Jesus in custody. Jesus had become a very dangerous man because Annas was a very wise interrogator, and yet he was unable to extract from Jesus anything that would allow him to build a case. That was a sorry action and work by this high priest to begin with—to have no case but to be seeking a case based on something incriminating that you can twist is an act of a lost man. Nevertheless, Jesus was in the custody of this sort of people.

He sought to gain some information to develop charges against Jesus, but the only thing he discovered was that he still lacked any legal justification for the arrest. And so we have an illegal arrest. We have an unproductive interview. And Jesus, he had now learned, would not be cowed just because he was bound and interrogated by a high priest, a revered high priest. So Annas had learned something about the character of his Prey as well.

His Prey would not be cowed simply because they had put him in a compromising position, simply because they were seeking to communicate that they had power and they had authority over his very life. Jesus still stood firmly and unwavering and unshaken because Jesus stands in the truth. Now while Jesus was with Annas—and that would be from 3:00 am until probably around daybreak—messengers had gone out seeking to round up the Sanhedrin, seeking to round up important witnesses so that they could come in and be coached and taught what they needed to say. Meanwhile Caiaphas was getting the assembly hall, the meeting, in order, answering questions, checking to make sure the witnesses were present and properly taught as to what they should speak.

We imagine that as Jesus walked in, it was still probably being brought to order. Remember, they were knocking on doors, and they were getting these priests up in the middle of the night before daybreak, assembling them for an important trial that was about to take place at daybreak because the trial could not occur at night. And so they brought Jesus in. The men were most likely sitting in a semi-circle. Jesus' eyes would have been able to survey and see all of those gathered against him. John leaves out the account of the actual trial, moving instead from Annas straight unto the interview with Pilate. But he doesn't neglect to mention that it occurred, and he reports for us the response of the Jews as a result of what was accomplished in the trial before the Sanhedrin with Caiaphas.

Some would try to combine those two trials—the one with Annas and the one with Caiaphas. They would say that Annas was simply at the trial and was the one doing the interview, but John makes it clear that that is not the case. He gives us a full report of the time with Annas, and then says Jesus was taken away from him to Caiaphas for the trial, and then removed from Caiaphas to Pilate. And so we know there were three—if you want to count the one with Annas as an actual trial—there were three times that Christ stood to answer questions concerning his person and his ministry.

In order to explore this trial with Caiaphas, we will need to supplement our understanding by the gospels, specifically Matthew, Chapter 26 which gives us an account of the trial.

> Then those who had seized Jesus led Him to Caiaphas the high priest, where the scribes and the elders had gathered. And Peter was following Him at a distance, as far as the courtyard of the high priest, and going inside he sat with the guards to see the end. Now the chief priests and the whole Council were seeking false testimony against Jesus that they might put Him to death, but they found none, though many false witnesses came forward. At last two came forward and said, 'This man said, "I am able to destroy the temple of God, and to rebuild it in three days."'
>
> And the high priest stood up and said, "Have you no answer to make? What is it that these men testify against you?" But Jesus remained silent. And the high priest said to him, "I adjure you by the living God, tell us if you are the Christ, the Son of God." Jesus said to him, "You have said so. But I tell you, from now on you will see the Son of Man seated at the right hand of Power and coming on the clouds of heaven." Then the high priest tore his robes and said, "He has uttered blasphemy. What further witnesses do we need? You have now heard his blasphemy. What is your judgment?" They answered, "He deserves death." Then they spit in His face and struck him. And some slapped Him, saying, "Prophesy to us, you Christ! Who is it that struck you?"

Maybe John fails to report the trial of Caiaphas because there was nothing really that could be accomplished. It only gave them opportunity to move the trial to Pilate. It only drove them deeper and deeper into their hatred. Whatever the reason, let's take a few moments, and let's mention just a few of the important details presented by the Synoptic writers.

The first point that cannot be lost on us is that Caiaphas represented the highest legal religious council in the world. That is where Jesus had been called. Let's get it out of our minds that this is some backroom dealing and Jesus was being handled by the Mob. That is not the case. This court, this assembling of the Sanhedrin, was the highest, purely religious court in the world at that time. Rome was the highest legal authority in the civil affairs of the world, but in the Sanhedrin we have represented a pure religious court made up of priests, scribes, and Pharisees.

Now that is a large statement, but it is a true statement. Where else is God's governing community to be found except in Israel? It was in Israel where God has established His people. It was in Israel where God has appointed priests. It was in Israel where sacrifices were made in the Temple. It was in Israel where the covenant of God was held, where his law was read, and it was in Israel where now the high priests gathered to try Christ. It was here that the highest religious court—I would say on this day the highest religious tribunal—had ever been held because at this trial God incarnate himself was standing before his own people in trial. It's a profound scene if you'll allow yourself to dwell upon that for a moment.

We often fly through the readings of the trials to the Cross, rightly emphasizing the atonement, rightly emphasizing the Cross; but think for just a moment that God Almighty was now standing on trial before his own people, and being held to account by his own Word, and being found guilty and deserving of death.

Nietzsche, the great philosopher, has nothing on this when he says, "God has died, and we simply haven't yet sounded the toll." The people of God holding God's own Word had declared God himself to be guilty and deserving of death. His own people had sought to kill their own God. If that doesn't represent the highest religious court to date in the world and in history, then nothing else will measure up.

The meaning of this court is that Jesus was being condemned by religious authority, and then later when he in Rome by secular authority, which means that there is no system of government invented by man and superintended by man that is freed from guilt and can say, "We wouldn't have done that." There is no system that man can develop where he can excuse himself and say, "Oh, if we had been there, we wouldn't have done that," or, "We would have done something different," because the Roman system has remained the model of the legal system which we follow today.

And we still hold to the law of God. It was under these two systems that Jesus was tried.

So where are we going to turn and say we would have done better, we would have been wiser, we wouldn't have done that, we would've created another system, He was a victim of circumstances? Those same circumstances are the circumstances we have this very day. Both our civil courts and our religious courts are still in existence today. Thank God, sitting on our religious courts, we hope are godly men and women so moved and changed by the Spirit of Christ that they wouldn't execute the same sentence. But nevertheless, we have religious courts. We have civil courts. And we even see some of the same back and forth. Sometimes a religious court arrives at a conviction, and then it is carried over into a civil court. We see some of these same patterns played out even today. This is not so backroom as we might imagine if we just quickly read through the trials of Christ.

Rome had granted the Sanhedrin authority to handle all matters within Judea. They didn't interfere. This was a high privilege. Rome had a great respect for the people of Israel concerning their religion, but they reserved to Rome some decisions, particularly concerning the death penalty. In the Jewish legal process, there wasn't a prosecutor like we know. There was not one who brought a case. The case was actually brought by the witnesses. That is why the witnesses were so important. The witnesses had to be there because the case had to be brought by these witnesses so that the Sanhedrin could then rule about the case. But we see all of this distorted in the motivation. They were seeking witnesses so they could justify a sentence they had already decided upon. They were seeking witnesses not to weigh the case impartially, but they were seeking witnesses to justify the death penalty which they had intended from the start.

Caiaphas, as he listened to these witnesses and the conflicting testimony could positively see the case crumbling away before him. The very people whom he would depend upon to make a case contradicted one another, and they were coming up with wilder, outrageous stories, things that couldn't be substantiated. There was still at the end of a parade of witnesses no legal ground to bring Christ even to trial, much less to convict him. But Caiaphas was a very smart man. He also knew his Scriptures, and he settled on a Maskil that Jesus had taught.

A Maskil is a saying that is given by one who is a teacher, particularly a prophet. It's a saying that is deliberately not explained. It can't be explained. If it is explained, it no longer is a Maskil. The purpose behind its not being explained is so that the people who listen have this wise saying for deep contemplation, meditation, and reflection. Jesus said, "Tear down this Temple, and in three days I will rebuild it." Now the Scriptures explain to us very clearly that Jesus was speaking about his own body, which is the temple. But he did not utter that in their hearing.

The Scriptures have other Maskils. Psalm 31:1: "In you, O LORD, do I take refuge; let me never be put to shame." What do we imagine when we hear the words "In You . . . I take refuge"? That is a saying that evokes in us some meditation, some contemplation—a word picture. Psalm 42:1: "As a deer pants for flowing streams, so pants my soul for You, O God." A saying for contemplation and for mediation. Jesus said, "Destroy this temple, and in three days I will raise it up."

Caiaphas decided to grab hold of that, and he demanded of Jesus an explanation. Jesus didn't explain the saying even though John has reported to us what it means concerning the resurrection. Jesus remained silent. Caiaphas tried to turn it into a charge, a charge against Jesus that he intended to destroy the Temple. This was a serious charge. We know from Jeremiah 26 that if anyone mentioned they would destroy the Temple, that was cause for death. There, Jeremiah was calling the people to repent while he was standing in the Temple. He called everyone into the Temple, and called them to repent, saying that if they didn't repent, the Temple, "this house," he calls it, will be made like Shiloh. In other words, it would be destroyed. Those who were gathered there sought to grab him, yelling that he was threatening to destroy the Temple, and for that threat he should die.

Jesus, in his role as a Prophet, had issued a Maskil, and Caiaphas demanded he explain it. If Jesus explained it, then he would discredit his own role as a Prophet. But if he didn't explain it, then he would leave them confounded as to a charge. So silence was the way to go.

The trial was still deadlocked. The court was deadlocked. Caiaphas, being a smart man, however unscrupulous, knew that the people expected the destruction of the current Temple in order for the Messiah to rebuild a more glorious one when he comes. So now he used the people's anticipation that the Temple would in fact be destroyed when Messiah comes, and he turns it. Luke faithfully records Jesus' response in 22, verse 67 and 68. He says, "If I tell you, you will not believe, and if I ask you, you will not answer. But from now on the Son of Man shall be seated at the right hand of the power of God." That was Jesus' response.

Caiaphas looked at him and said, "Explain to us what you mean by this." Jesus said to him, "If I tell you what I mean, you're not going to believe it, and if I ask you a question, you're not going to answer it. But I'll tell you what you will see. You will see the Son of Man seated at the right hand of power." What did Jesus mean regarding a question he might ask? He had already confronted them with a decision about him back in Matthew 22.

> Now while the Pharisees were gathered together, Jesus asked them a question, saying, "What do you think about the Christ? Whose Son is He?" They said to him, "The Son of David." He said to them, "How is it then that David, in the Spirit, calls him Lord, saying, "The Lord said to my Lord, 'Sit at my right hand, until I put your enemies under your feet'? If then David calls him Lord, how is He his Son?" And no one was able to answer him a word, nor from that day did anyone dare to ask him any more questions." (Matthew 22:41 to 46)

Yes, they will not believe, nor will they reason with him about his questions.

They asked him questions. If he answered, they wouldn't believe. If he asked them questions to arrive at truth, then they became silent and wouldn't answer. Caiaphas wanted more than this however. He wasn't satisfied with Jesus' answer because if Jesus confessed to be the Messiah, charges of treason could be drawn up as treason against the king, against Rome, against Caesar. If Jesus confessed to be the Son of God, then charges of heresy could be drawn up, and those charges resulted in death.

Matthew 26, verse 63 records Caiaphas playing his last card. He called Jesus to swear by an oath to the living God. "I adjure you . . ." he says, ". . . by the living God, tell us if you are the Christ, the Son of God." This had to be a painful question for Jesus. Caiaphas called him to swear an oath in God's name, as if everything Jesus had said, everything Jesus had prayed, everything Jesus had taught was not before the living God. He now called upon Jesus to tell the truth, implying that Jesus had not told the truth.

If Jesus answered no, there were no charges. He had to be released. Think about that a moment. He said, "I adjure you by the living God, tell us if you are the Christ, the Son of God." If Jesus said no, everything was over. But if Jesus said yes, the plan to have him killed would go forward. Caiaphas had now brought it to a crisis point. Jesus had avoided awakening the nationalistic and political energies of the Jews by identifying with their ambitions for a Messiah throughout his whole ministry. He had not made much about his call of Messiah, but now Jesus was under oath by the judge of the highest religious court of the world, a people established by God himself, and given authority. And this authority had now placed Christ himself under oath to tell the truth. He could not be silent before this challenge to his person, to his purpose, and to his being.

So in Matthew 26:64 we read, "Jesus said to him, 'You have said so. But I tell you, from now on you will see the Son of Man seated at the right hand of Power and coming on the clouds of heaven.'" Jesus here affirmed two prophecies to present himself to Caiaphas. One from Daniel, chapter 7, verse 13 which describes the Son of Man as coming with clouds and from heaven, and the other is from David's Psalm 110, verse 1 where the Lord said to my Lord, sit at my right hand. Both are considered messianic, and here Jesus claimed to share in divine power.

Daniel's vision I think is particularly profound. In Daniel, chapter 7, verse 2: "In my vision at night I looked, and there before me were the four winds of heaven churning up the great sea. Four great beasts . . . came up out of the sea." And then Daniel 7:13: "In my vision at night I looked, and there before me was one like a son of man, coming with the clouds. . . ." Jesus made reference to this vision, to this prophecy in Daniel. The dream came in the first year of Belshazzar the king of Babylon. Daniel was under great distress because of the state of Israel, and God showed him that every swing of the pendulum in history and in life remains under the jurisdiction and the providence of God, that he is never out of control, that the future belongs to God, even as Assyria, or even as Babylon, or even as Medo-Persia are raised up, and Israel will be made to suffer at their hand, even in those cases that it is God who raised them up. It is God who gave them might and power and authority, and that Daniel should not ever believe that God is no longer the caretaker of his people.

In that vision, there are four creatures that arise from the sea that represent four successive kingdoms—Babylon, the Medo-Persian Empire, the Macedonian Empire, and the Roman Empire. Without getting a lot into the different empires, let's ask, why the sea? Why do they rise out of the sea? What is the picture of the sea?

These days when the ocean is in the news, we often get pictures of tsunamis and rogue waves, and we see them crashing into piers and ships, but then they go away. They're powerful and they're mighty and they're large. If you've stood on the shore and watched as large waves begin to swell up and crash, by the time they reach your feet, there is nothing but a little foam and a little ripple, and then they recede back out into the sea where they came from.

Here we have a picture of great beasts rising up out of the sea. Everything that comes from the sea flows back to the sea as if it never were. Contrary to that vision of these earthly kingdoms that rise up and then disappear back where they came from, he looks up and sees from the clouds the Son of Man who is coming down from the heavens—from the heavens which are eternal, which are not like the sea, which are set and which are established. He looks to the sky, and there is a visible kingdom that cannot be moved, and between the eternal rest of heaven's salvation and the turbulent tragedy of this world stands a Mediator, the Son of Man.

If Caiaphas had ears to hear, he might have been struck dead with fear because Jesus told him, "The next time you see me, I will be sitting as divine Judge at your trial. When you see me, you will see the Son of Man coming in glory and in judgment." In saying this, Jesus proved that he is the highest Prophet and Teacher by interpreting the Old Testament Scriptures. Rather than preserving the riddle of Daniel, he showed them that the prophecy of Daniel was about him. They were now in the New Testament which was about to be written in his blood.

In Caiaphas' estimation however, they had all they needed. The death penalty was decided upon. Jesus claimed to be the Son of God in such a unique sense that he was sharing in God's divine power. This is the story behind John 1:11. He came to his own, and his own people did not receive him. Jesus had bested them in every encounter, but today they thought was their day. And as they rose to leave, they spat on the Lord as a sign of their contempt. Some began hitting and slapping him. Maybe since they couldn't stone him to death which was what their law required, they felt emboldened to do this instead. They blindfolded him and taunted him as they struck him, challenging him to guess at who was hitting him, since he was a Prophet.

One thing this proves is that they understood Jesus was before them in his prophetic capacity, and they rejected his prophecy. There was no confusion. They understood he was standing before them as a Prophet, and so they teased, and jeered at him, and said, "Okay, prophet, then tell us who hit you."

There is no record of Jesus ducking. No record of him calling out. No record of him protesting or pushing back. How often had he seen this before in his own mind's eye? He told the disciples in Mark, chapter 10, "See, we are going up to Jerusalem, and the Son of Man will be delivered over to the chief priests and the scribes, and they will condemn him to death and deliver him over to the Gentiles. And they will mock him and spit on him, and flog him and kill him. And after three days he will rise."

Even centuries before, Isaiah described the exact scene which we just read, in chapter 50. "I gave my back to those who strike, and my cheeks to those who pull out the beard; I hid not my face from disgrace and spitting." What shame we share for man. We don't know how long this went on. We don't know how badly Jesus was beaten by the mob. We know he only waited the coming dawn of the day that changed all of history.

The sentence of death for blasphemy was required by the law of Moses, but the sentence could not be carried out by the Jews. And so as the sun rose, Jesus would be turned over by his own people to the Roman procurator named Pilate. By his silence, Christ showed them that he was a true Prophet. By his speech, he showed them the divine nature of the Messiah. There are a couple of reflections worth considering.

The first comes from his silence before the Sanhedrin. At first, we might be puzzled about why he wouldn't speak. Why won't he explain himself? Why not teach, even if it's just for our benefit? Why not speak and maybe even offer them an opportunity to believe? But they had heard. They knew his teaching. And now their guilt was for them alone to seal. They had heard it all. They were there. In fact, Jesus' own testimony says, "You've already heard." And now all that was left was for them to make a decision to seal their own guilt.

How many times do those who have heard the message of grace continue to ask for an answer that they already possess? What is left for us to say? What is left for us to teach? What have we withheld? What do we keep secret? Nothing. Nothing! How many Bible stores do we need? How many mail order catalogs have to offer the Scriptures? How many audio cassettes or CDs have to be published? How many radio stations have to go on air? How many churches have to preach the saving gospel of Jesus Christ? How many answers have not been provided? None. And still it's not enough. It's not enough for the heart that is already decided not to believe.

The second is that when Jesus did answer, his answer was the promise of the judgment to come, and on the promise of deliverance, we should take particular note. Isn't this the place we all have to come to eventually? Will Jesus be your Messiah, or will Jesus come in glory as the Son of Man as your Judge? Will he be your salvation, or will he be the One to declare your condemnation?

I will conclude this chapter with an observation: there are two extremes that proved inadequate in today's court case. On the one hand, there may be those who can't know Jesus and don't know the revelation of Jesus in Scripture. There are those who don't know him because they don't study the Scripture. How can you possibly say you believe in One whom you don't know? So there is the arrogance of ignorance on the one hand. One who would say, "Oh, I can believe without being introduced to the One whom I profess to believe in."

And then on the other hand, there are those who are like Caiaphas. They have the Scriptures, they've studied the Scriptures, they know the Scriptures, but they are so inebriated with a love for themselves that they cannot hear the Christ of the Scriptures, and they turn their backs on Jesus. Many today ignore the testimony of the Church concerning Christ. They won't read, they won't listen, they won't attend, they have very short patience for the presentation of the gospel, they're bored with it more times than not, and so we can say they are not seeking truth. Rather, they're seeking an excuse.

And so what about you? You're reading Christ's own defense of himself. You hold the Scriptures in your hands. Now you have his testimony. His trial is over. Ours has just begun. What do you say about this Jesus?

7

Jesus the Outlaw

John 18:24, 28–32

> Annas then sent him bound to Caiaphas the high priest. . . . Then they led Jesus from the house of Caiaphas to the governor's headquarters. It was early morning. They themselves did not enter the governor's headquarters, so that they would not be defiled, but could eat the Passover. So Pilate went outside to them and said, "What accusation do you bring against this man?" They answered him, "If this man were not doing evil, we would not have delivered him over to you." Pilate said to them, "Take him yourselves and judge him by your own law." The Jews said to him, "It is not lawful for us to put anyone to death." This was to fulfill the word that Jesus had spoken to show by what kind of death he was going to die.

In John, chapter 18, we read about the Gentile trial, the trial before Pilate. You recall we have completed the inquisition before Annas. Peter heard the cock crow because he had come to the conclusion of his own denials. And Jesus was now being carried off to a trial with Pilate for the purposes of being executed.

Some might wonder if John's accounts conflict with the other gospels by suggesting that the Sanhedrin were still in a pre-Passover time because when they delivered Jesus we're told that they didn't want to go inside for fear of being defiled and unable to partake of the Passover celebration. Yet, haven't we already read that Jesus and his disciples had celebrated the Passover meal? This is easily reconciled because Passover is more than just the feast and a lamb in the life of ancient Israel there in Jerusalem.

There were a number of festivities that went along with a Passover celebration, so it's easy to understand how they could have very well had a Passover meal but still had been in the midst of a Passover celebration. And the rules for ceremonial cleanliness were binding for the activities even after the Paschal lamb was served.

The scruples of the Sanhedrin at the doorway of Pilate show us the conflict that they were experiencing with the externalization of the law. We have a shorthand way of describing that. It's called *legalism*, and their true spiritual fulfillment of the law evaded them. It wouldn't take much to develop a treatment of the grave circumstances of that extravagant sin they were committing by delivering Jesus to Pilate even while they were so careful to observe the small issues, believing that in doing so they were somehow keeping themselves clean. It's an example of those who would strain at the gnat while swallowing the camel.

The Church still struggles with that even to this day. How else can a sinner pretend self-righteousness except to ignore the real and deep and broad spiritual meaning and focus instead on the minor, legalistic, or contrived issues? Their religion was externalized by form. Jesus is the form and the substance of the law. We must be careful not to become accidentally Pharisaical because it's so easy to stop and say, "Oh, I can't step inside. I'll be ceremonially unclean." And yet how hard is it to say, "In the spirit of Christ, it is not about me. It is about my Lord"?

In their action to deliver Christ, a great change occurs in the economy of salvation. Instead of separating themselves from pagan palaces, we are now called to separate ourselves from the essence of sin. They simply believed they would not be sinners if they didn't step into the palace. We are now called not simply to not step into the palace. We are called to be separated from sin. Oddly however, it was the legislative separation that caused them to need to turn Jesus over to Pilate. Isn't that interesting? Their concern about the law is what drove them to turn over the Lamb who takes away the sin of the world even while they were staying clean to observe Passover. They were sending away the Passover Lamb which they would need for their own salvation while they were observing the tenets of the law in their faith. What they intended for evil, God used for good.

Jerusalem, along with Judea as a whole, was classified by Rome as subject territory. That is why Pilate would say to them, "Carry him off, and judge him by your own law. You judge him, and you punish him according to the way that you see fit." A subject territory is one where Rome reserved right to intervene in whatever Rome deemed necessary, but one in which Rome ordinarily left the residents to their own local government within their own courts. In particular, the Jews of Alexandria and Asia Minor enjoyed autonomy.

Now this is important because the Jews had tried, and often would try, and these since 49 BC enjoyed so much autonomy under Rome that they could even try citizens of Rome, albeit without executing the death penalty. If a Roman citizen, as we have record that some did—particularly Roman guards and centurions—if they offended the Jewish law, then the Jews were allowed to try them. So the Jewish court was allowed a great deal of latitude and a great deal of authority in Jerusalem and Asia Minor. The privileges extended to Jews included exemption from military duty and exemption from the emperor worship which so typified citizens of Rome.

For all practical purposes, the only limitation reserved to Rome was the sentence of death. This helps us explain why Pilate was willing to come out at such an hour to the Jews who were there. We know that he actually despised those Jews who were in Jerusalem. He came to Jerusalem in times of high festivals and feasts and stayed there in the Fortress of Antonia because he needed to supervise and oversee the Jews in times like that so that they wouldn't rebel and there wouldn't be an overthrow of the Roman yoke.

The Fortress of Antonia stood at the highest point within the city, the Temple stood at the next highest, and then Jerusalem proper. That is also significant because the Temple was a fortress overlooking Jerusalem, and wherever the people were, they would look up and they would see the Temple. But when Herod became tetrarch, and when Herod was there, not only did he want to get out of the residence where his mother-in-law lived, but he also wanted to build a fortress that was a little bit higher so that he could have authority and rule over Jerusalem. And so he built up higher this Fortress of Antonia.

There would be ramparts that would come down. If you were to picture it in your eye, you would see perhaps one large tower with four towers on the sides. The ramparts extended down into the temple, and guards were able to patrol and keep watch over everything that happened in the Temple and in the streets. So from that perch, Pilot is able to squash any rebellion that may have occurred.

It's odd that they would give a people they so distrust so much latitude, but traditionally the Jews had been allowed a great deal of self-rule and autonomy. The thought is that the emperor who initially gave the Jews

Jesus the Outlaw   63

this autonomy lived by the principle that just like flies on a carcass, once they've had their fill, they demand no more. And so he sort of saw the Jews with the same sort of disdain, not respect, but thinking that the best way to keep them quiet was to give them enough of what they wanted, and then they wouldn't seek to rebel anymore.

If the Sanhedrin wanted the death penalty, Pilate thought, *then that had to be exercised by Rome.* The Sanhedrin, being the highest religious court, and having that much autonomy could sway the people and could cause rebellion. So Pilate because he was the governor came out to meet this highest court. Here we have a picture of what the Sanhedrin feared losing. They needed to be rid of Jesus because if Jesus did cause a messianic movement to occur, then there could be a rebellion against Rome. These Jewish leaders were beholden to Rome. They had sold out to Rome, and Rome had established them in their power.

It's odd isn't it that the people who were the leaders of the Jews now actually were the taskmasters of Rome? They were the ones who were the Roman puppets. They were the ones who kept the Jews under control for Rome, and their power was established by Rome. So instead of liberation when Jesus comes, he would cause them to lose their position and their authority and their respectability, and so their eyes were so blinded that they could not see Jesus as the true Messiah. I would submit—and I believe that there are enough quotes from Pharisees and the Sanhedrin to back this up—that they actually suspected that Jesus could be the Messiah, but unless Jesus could demonstrate a power equal to Rome and guarantee their own authority, they preferred to keep their standing under Rome rather than risk losing it under God's rule.

Jesus, in being brought to Pilate, was being cast outside of the Jewish civil, the Jewish ceremonial, and the Jewish ethical, or moral, code. He was being made an outlaw in the sense of being excommunicated from everything Jewish. In the courts, laws were broken. Jesus was brought to trial illegally. They tried to find trumped-up charges against him, so there were illegal charges brought against him. The act of striking him was even illegal as it was illegal to strike a man who had not yet been found guilty.

Now he was being removed from the protection of the Mosaic law altogether and being thrown outside of the nation of Israel into the courts of the Gentiles. Jesus had been excommunicated, thrown out of the nation, delivered to the Gentiles, but the Gentile world cares little for the law of God just as the Church today is captive to the laws of a secular nation while the nation refuses to acknowledge even the moral law.

Isn't it interesting if you think just a moment about how so many of us rightfully care for, support, love our national cause and our Constitution and all things that are American, and yet America refuses to even post the Ten Commandments of our God? We do live in a two-kingdom world. We do live in subjection to the authority over us, but we must be careful also or else we become like the Sanhedrin. In a quest to hold onto position, we rely not upon God, but upon a nation and upon the benefits that a political power can give.

Pilate would have ordinarily thought very little about respecting the Jewish verdict because that would be the pattern throughout history. He respected what the Sanhedrin could do, but he had no respect for Jewish law. He had no respect for Jewish authority. No respect for Jewish scruples or the God of the Jewish nation. We find this in the rest of Scripture. In Corinth, for example, the Jews approached Gallio to have Paul declared an heretic, and he said in Acts 18, "If it were a matter of wrongdoing or vicious crime, O Jews, I would have reason to accept your complaint. But since it is a matter of questions about words and names and your own law, see to it yourselves. I refuse to be a judge of these things."

Years later, in Acts 23, Paul is taken by the Roman tribune under its protective custody because he decided the Jewish charges were issues of Jewish law and not punishable by death under Roman law. The tribune just took him away and said, "You folks are trying this man, but your law is nothing at all to be even respected." In Acts 25, Festus showed no real interest in putting Paul to trial over Jewish offenses, saying in verse 20, "I am at a loss as to how to investigate these questions." In other words, he is at unable to find any legal standing for the complaints which the Jews bring.

A secular world has no foundation or basis on which to even weigh or measure the concerns of the Lord because our concerns are concerns of the soul, concerns that are with the idea of eternity and with the glory of God. How can a secular court weigh those concerns and bring a just decision? History concludes that Rome allowed the Jews a remarkable amount of self-governance, but Rome herself didn't make much out of Jewish law. Rome allowed the death penalty for crimes against Jewish religious rites. Blasphemy was not such a crime. Blasphemy was not a law for which Rome would have allowed for the death penalty, so they declared Jesus a non-Jew, an outlaw, and a heretic.

But Pilate was not going to be one to give a rubber stamp. Pilate was going to have to examine this himself. If they could have proved that Jesus planned to destroy the Temple, that would have qualified for a quick sentence by Pilate because the law did protect Jewish architecture. The law did protect against sacrilege against Jewish worship services. But blasphemy? Blasphemy against the God of the Jews was not blasphemy against the gods of Rome. Rome didn't worship the God of the Jews, and so it didn't merit death by Roman law. This is why blasphemy was replaced with an emphasis on high treason as the crime because that *was* against Roman law.

That is one reason we would distinguish between the religious trial for blasphemy in claiming to be the unique Son of God, and the civil trial which he was about to undergo, which was concerned with the Lordship in the kingdom of Christ.

We wonder what use the Jewish trial was if the verdict was toothless. There were at least two practical outcomes from that trial. Being the highest religious tribunal, their verdict implied a great moral offense. In John 19:7, they reminded Pilate of the moral pressure and authority they brought, saying, "We have a law, and according to that law he ought to die because he has made himself the Son of God." The Sanhedrin brought pressure on Pilate, saying, "We have a law, and he ought to die according to that law." And Pilate heard them.

The second is that such a dramatic sentence would draw in a nationalistic and local passion that Pilate would hear as a popular demand for the execution. So the Sanhedrin made a very savvy political and ungodly play. They brought forward a charge, thinking that in that charge they could whip up a public sentiment that would carry Jesus to the Cross, or to stoning which was actually the means of death under Jewish law.

They were trying to manipulate the crowds by bringing something that got their interest. The claim to be the unique Son of God, they believed would be just that issue. That would mobilize the people. Then they reminded Pilate, "Oh, by the way, this is against our law and is punishable by death." So Pilate heard that the Sanhedrin said Jesus' crime was punishable by death, and then also the very charge itself got the people of Jerusalem excited. So now Pilate was more or less forced into some sort of action.

Klaas Schilder, who wrote a great trilogy on the Passion, says, "This therefore is the piteous state of things. Israel turns to the world for assistance in destroying its own Redeemer. In short, Israel returns to the house of bondage. Israel goes back to Egypt."[1]

If Pilate had arrived just before Passover in Jerusalem, we can be fairly certain his intention was to prevent any such nationalistic riot among the crowds. It was this secular, this worldly motivated, this carnal judge whom the religious leadership now turned to as their authority to help to accomplish their will. They didn't turn to the nation. They didn't turn to the Law of Moses. They turned to secular authority to accomplish their will.

Anyone spending any time in Scripture will quickly note the repeated contrast between the people of God and the world. The people of God, alternately called the *elect*, the *chosen*, a *holy nation*, a *peculiar people*, or *Christian*, are never instructed to mix with the world, that is, the way of the world. Romans 12:2: "Do not be conformed to this world, but be transformed by the renewal of your mind."

First John, chapter 4, verses 5 and 6 describe the substantial difference in thinking between the people of God and the people of the world. There John says, "They are from the world; therefore they speak from the world, and the world listens to them. We are from God. Whoever knows God listens to us; whoever is not from God does not listen to us. By this we know the Spirit of truth and the spirit of error." It's not simply a matter of the world not subscribing to the Christian faith. The world cannot grasp the Christian faith. The world cannot make judgments based upon the Christian faith. The world's judgments come from a different paradigm, and it is not a neutral paradigm.

All through Israel's history, God had taught them to be separated out from the world, whether it was in leaving Egypt for the Promised Land, or refraining from marriage to unbelievers, or direct restrictions, or it was circumcision, or it was baptism. God tells his people that a little leaven will corrupt the entire loaf, and bad company corrupts good morals. Even going back to the Garden, we're taught that there is a chosen Seed of the woman who is predestined to redeem and the seed of Satan who is predestined to resist.

---

1. Schilder, *Christ on Trial*, 223.

Since that time, there has been a conflict between the empire of the world and the kingdom of God, whether it's found in Cain and Abel, Israel and the Philistines, Jesus and the Sanhedrin, or Jesus and Rome, or the Church and Satan. Wherever it is found, we know the conflict persists. When God gave Israel the Commandments, he began by reminding them of this, "I am the LORD your God, who brought you out of the land of Egypt, out of the house of slavery."

God sent Moses to lead the people out following that evening when the angel of death descended and only skipped those homes where the blood of the Paschal lamb was placed on the doorpost. This was the opening act of a long, historic drama of God's rescue of his people from slavery and bondage of Satan and the kingdom of the world. Even in this opening act, however, the people quickly wanted to return to the secular world that they had already known so well. God sovereignly pushed them forward driven by Pharaoh's army, like a great herd being driven by herdsman. And then he led them on by fire and cloud. Then so that they would not wander far, he himself fed them in the wilderness.

Still on multiple occasions, the people forfeited their blessings, and they married other nations. They compromised God's law. They became lovers of self rather than lovers of God. Over and again, Israel chose the natural over the supernatural. They choose sight over faith. They choose the world over heaven. They choose servitude over freedom. Jesus came announcing that once for all he would set the captives free. And again, the people of God's choosing turn, or return, to the world, to the yoke of bondage rather than the light yoke of the Messiah. The high priest begs Rome to take away the burden of God himself from them. How ironic that the religious leader would beg the world to take God away from them. The priesthood of Israel was not of the Spirit; it was of the flesh.

After these Jewish leaders so carefully observe their ceremonial cleanliness, Pilate will go through all the motions of seeking justice, while in the end allowing a mob to determine the verdict. Pilate now stands for Egypt as Israel goes back to eat from Pharaoh's hand. The Jews ask Pharaoh in the person of Pilate to liberate them from the One who is greater than Moses. But in their hour of tragedy, they cast a seed that opens a way of salvation for the world. While Israel decides to give up her place as the spiritual people of God and become one of the many nations, they open the way for a greater kingdom and a people too numerous to count.

Have you in your life had an epiphany, a moment where there was clarity? A moment where you could see? Have you had a time in your life when Jesus has come so near, and spiritual life was imparted to you? Have you tasted the grace of the Holy Spirit and known the sweet fellowship of his Church? And having done all of this, have you ever been tempted, or God forbid, returned to the mire of carnal living that you were called away from?

Have you longed more for the hand of Pharaoh than Christ? Have you sought your freedom in walking away from Christ instead of walking with him? Have you found his commandments to be burdensome instead of liberating? Take care that your own religion is not the religion of the Pharisees. The Pharisees and the Sanhedrin can be described by the saying in Hosea 6, "For I desire steadfast love and not sacrifice, the knowledge of God rather than burnt offerings. But like Adam they transgressed the covenant; there they dealt faithlessly with me." This is why Jesus said of the Pharisees in Luke 16, "You are those who justify yourselves before men, but God knows your hearts. For what is exalted among men is an abomination in the sight of God."

May these words never apply to any of us. Walk with Christ in humility and self-sacrificial love. Die to the things of this world rather than strive for them. Bless rather than curse. Be a man and woman of substance rather than form. Don't return to the ease of Egypt; the yoke of Christ is light and the burden is not heavy. Fear Egypt. Fear the world and the kingdom Satan, not the kingdom of Christ.

8

Once a King . . .

John 18:33–36

> So Pilate entered his headquarters again and called Jesus and said to him, "Are you the King of the Jews?" Jesus answered, "Do you say this of your own accord, or did others say it to you about me?" Pilate answered, "Am I a Jew? Your own nation and the chief priests have delivered you over to me. What have you done?" Jesus answered, "My kingdom is not of this world. If my kingdom were of this world, my servants would have been fighting, that I might not be delivered over to the Jews. But my kingdom is not from the world."

On Palm Sunday almost all of Christendom celebrates the triumphal entry of Christ, celebrates his arrival into Jerusalem. We also, acknowledging that arrival, will continue to deal with the question of kingdom for that is what his triumphal entry was all about. The King had come into his city. And we know that as he arrived at that city, he also wept, for the city did not recognize the arrival of their King. That issue of his kingship, his being King, continues to be vetted now in his trial with Pilate as he continues to discover that there is a lack of understanding not only among the Jews, but now also among the Gentiles as they are represented in the person of Pilate.

If you want to get involved in an intense and often divisive debate, bring up the topic of your view of the kingdom of God, and when and how it arrives or whether it already has arrived. Ask someone if a king needs a kingdom. Can Jesus be a King if there is not actually a kingdom now? If so, is he a King in exile? Is Jesus in exile sitting at the right hand of God, or is Jesus reigning over a kingdom?

Some understand the kingdom of God as being present and visible, with an emphasis being upon visible, that is, present in this world with a right of rule even over the civil magistrate or civil government. This is certainly the position of Rome. Historically, Rome has asserted pressure on kings and sovereigns. There was the Holy Roman Empire. As part of their governance and rule, they collected taxes, and they even waged war.

Some have replaced the theology of the kingdom of God with this emphasis on witness, covenant, and—yes—judgment with a social gospel, choosing to establish a kingdom based upon a social work in this world and in this time. Some understand the kingdom as something that is still future. They don't see any reason to view the kingdom as something that is present or in the present tense, but instead they're awaiting the return of Christ and a literal, thousand-year millennial reign which will then be established. So until that time, there is no actual kingdom. In that view, while most would probably balk at the description, they have to adopt a view that if Jesus is King, he is indeed in exile, for his kingdom is not here.

Still others, to which most Reformed and Covenantal thinkers belong, teach that the kingdom is in fact very present and that it is spiritual in nature, and it awaits only the judgment at the second coming of Christ, at his parousia, for consummation. That is the language that is so typically used.

It gets rather hilarious as there are people who might describe themselves as pre-mil, as historic pre-mil, pre-mil, post-trib, post-mil, amil, and then of course pan-mil. That is the group who call themselves pan-millenialists who choose not to worry too much about how the kingdom will come because they assume it will all "pan out" in the end.

The concept of the kingdom is essential if we are to understand the gospel. We can't disregard it. We can't ignore it. We can't say that this only belongs to the halls of seminaries and theological giants because our idea of the kingdom will be how we express the gospel. We can't separate the two. Our understanding of the kingdom of God gives expression to our presentation of the gospel. The phrase *kingdom of God* is usually in both the Old Testament and in Jesus' teaching connected with coming judgment; therefore there is a sense of urgency in the work of the Church that holds to a strong kingdom theology because of the impending judgment that comes along with the kingdom of God. It's so central to our understanding that we regularly pray, "Thy kingdom come, Thy will be done in earth, as it is in heaven," committing ourselves to the idea that as God through Christ is ruling in the heavens, so that same rule would find expression here among his people. If we're going to take the gospel seriously, we have to take the Church seriously and understand the kingdom of God as it finds expression in the Church.

Then we need to understand the answers that Jesus gave to Pilate in John 18:36, when he said simply, "My kingdom is not of this world." Does that mean his kingdom is not in this world, or that his kingdom is quantifiably and qualitatively different from this world—the word *world* being used as an expression of the present tense, physical governments of this world? Our Westminster Confession of Faith isn't silent on the issue of kingdom. In chapter 30, in paragraph one and two, the entire structure of our church government and authority of the church rests on the very real and present kingdom of God. In other words, if the church is to have any authority in life and over the members of the church, it depends not upon the consent of the governed, but upon the kingdom of God and the authority of God, which is then passed to the church to rule.

In chapter 30, the first paragraph: "The Lord Jesus, as King and Head of his Church, hath therein appointed government, in the hand of Church officers, distinct from the civil magistrate." So here we find the teaching concerning the Church that there is a government that is distinct from the civil government. We might see a separation of Church and State, though we don't mean that the moral law of God has no influence or place in the civil government of man, but we're saying there should be no confusion between the government that belongs to the Church of our Lord Jesus Christ, who is King and Head, and the government which man has created and organized for his own governing of society.

It continues in paragraph two, "To these officers the keys of the kingdom of heaven are committed, by virtue whereof, they have power, respectively, to retain, and remit sins; to shut that kingdom against the impenitent, both by the Word, and censures when an occasion shall require." These powers are not notional powers. This is not figurative language. This is very real and specific language concerning not the privileges of those who are in leadership in the church, but the commission that is handed to them by God who is sovereign over his people and has established Christ Jesus as King who has committed to the Church, as his

Body in unity with him, the power and authority that belong to the reign of Christ in his kingdom.

If we don't accept that the kingdom is present, then we have a grace period—an interesting use of the word *grace*, given that we are excusing ourselves from the authority of God in his rule over his people. The writers of the Westminster Confession base the authority of the Church on the reality of the present kingdom of God.

So the question for us is this—*what difference does it make whether the kingdom is present now or coming later?* In the Lord's Prayer, we acknowledge it has to do with obedience to God's will. "Thy will be done in earth, as it is in heaven." And so we can understand that in the most practical sense if the kingdom is present, then we must be an obedient people. That is in fact what we have prayed. "Lord, make your will to be accomplished on earth just as it is in heaven."

In the most practical sense, we can look at Matthew 6:25 through 34. In these verses we are exhorted not to worry about clothing, not to worry about what we will eat or drink. Jesus presses the issue, pointing out God's providence over the natural world and charges them with having too little faith, making them act like the Gentile unbelievers of the world who do worry about their clothing, who do worry about what they will eat. And as Jesus concludes this teaching about their anxiety as being a symptom of a lack of trust in a sovereign and providential God, he says, "Seek first the kingdom of God and his righteousness, and all these things will be added to you." Seek first the kingdom of God. So is our obedience measured by a perpetual seeking with no expectation of finding, or should we expect that in seeking the kingdom it can be found?

Or to put it another way, does seeking separate us from unbelievers, or does finding separate us from unbelievers? I think if you ponder that, you'll find fundamentally that it is a way of describing most Christian experience. Are we separate because we are going to church seeking the kingdom, and they just don't? So therefore we can be a people who might not seek this Sunday because we were seeking last Sunday, and we'll come back and we'll seek again next Sunday. We're looking for it. We can't be expected to be looking all the time. Or are we a people with a citizenship and an obligation to gather because God has commanded us to gather? It all depends if the King is present or yet to come.

If the King is present, then we dare not forsake the assembling that is required, that is commanded by our King. But if he is yet to come, then certainly he will appreciate our transitory seeking, our seasonal seeking, our looking today and not looking tomorrow because if we look just a little bit, then that shows we have an interest in the arrival of the kingdom. But if the kingdom is already here, then how does it make us appear? We appear to be a people who are wishy-washy, who are double-minded, who are not yet ready to leave the world and to enter into the gates of the kingdom of God.

On Palm Sunday when Jesus rode triumphantly into Jerusalem as her King, was he really her King, or was he still simply an heir to the throne? If the people were hushed and the rocks cried out, would creation testify to his potential or to his arrival? What would have happened if the rocks had cried out? Would they have cried out, "The King is arrived!" or would they have cried out, "See, Jerusalem, your King who will come!"?

In the spring of 1935, Charles Harold Dodd, or as he is more commonly known in his writings *C. H. Dodd*, gave a series of lectures at Yale Divinity School looking closely at all the parables of Jesus as they related to the kingdom. I'll just mention a few of them.

The Parable of the talents is a kingdom parable. The parable of the sower and the four soils is a kingdom parable. The parable of the ten virgins with the lamps is a kingdom parable. When looking at the parables of Jesus as a whole, Dodd says, "Was all this wealth of loving observation and imaginative rendering of nature and common life used merely to adorn moral generalities? Was the Jesus of the gospels just an eminently sound and practical teacher who patiently led simple minds to appreciate the great enduring commonplaces of morals and religion? This is not the impression conveyed by the gospels as a whole."[1]

In other words, he is asking, "Were the parables Jesus taught simply to teach a Christian ethic, simply to convey a moral way of life? Were they examples, were they allegories to show us how we ought to understand and perceive the ethic and the law of God and of God's grace, or were they intended to communicate the actual establishment of the kingdom of God?"

I hope that at this point you're beginning to realize at least this: that whichever side you fall on that question will direct how you live your life as a Christian. Just how seriously do you take the gospel, just how seriously do you take the lordship of Christ, just how seriously do you take

---

1. Dodd, *Parables of the Kingdom*, 13.

the Church, even the church to which you have given vows unto the Lord of membership?

Think for a moment of how many times Jesus began his teaching with the words, "The kingdom of heaven is like. . . ." It's like a seed growing in secret. It's like leaven with which a little will affect the entire loaf. It's like a great feast, or a costly pearl, or a dragnet, or laborers in the vineyard. Jesus' entire ministry seemed to focus on the concept of communicating the truths about the kingdom, the kingdom of God.

This much we can say then, from the opening of Jesus' ministry, when John preached, "Repent, for the kingdom of God is at hand," a sentiment and a message which Jesus himself repeated. In Samaria Jesus told the Samaritan woman that the time is accomplished and the kingdom of God is at hand; through the triumphal entry and the interrogation before Pilate, Jesus centered himself on the proclamation of the kingdom. Regrettably, in our presentation of the gospel, you will rarely hear reference to the kingdom of God, and yet Jesus found that the gospel itself was simply the vessel from which the message of the kingdom was sent.

Our first application is that if we are to understand the sum of Jesus' teaching and the gospel itself, we must understand the kingdom. That brings to us a couple of questions if we're going to understand it. It's one thing to say you must understand it; another to actually understand it. We would say, "What kind of kingdom is it? Is this a kingdom that we can see? Is this a kingdom that is supposed to change the world in which we live? Is it a secret kingdom? Is it an invisible kingdom? What exactly are we talking about when we say the kingdom of God is present?" Whenever two or more are gathered, Jesus is there with them. Is he there with them because his kingdom is present, or is that a special visitation only in those times of worship?

The word *kingdom* points to some place or some community that is governed by a king in the most basic sense. If we say that there is a kingdom, we mean that there is something, some place that must exist. A real kingdom does not exist as an idea alone. There *must* be a kingdom. Even the Aramaic term *malcuth*, used so frequently by the Jews, means *kingly rule* or *reign* or *sovereignty*. How can there be a king if there is no rule? How can there be a king if there is no reign, if there is no sovereignty over his people? So to say *kingdom of God* means that God is reigning as a King, just as in the prayer when we say, "Thy will be done in earth, as it is in heaven." But those who listened to Jesus struggled because the signs of a kingdom ruled by God were not so clearly discernable in their time. They struggled with Jesus' message because the kingdom was not arriving in the way they expected it to arrive; with a righteous King comes both freedom for the oppressed and justice, that is judgment, against the oppressors.

John the Baptist showed us the tension emerging in Jesus' teaching when he asked in Matthew 11 whether Jesus is the One all of Jewish history has been anticipating, or if there was One who was yet to come. John's confusion resulted from his own expectation. He rightly discerned that there would be blessing that comes with the kingdom and also judgment to come with the kingdom. And he was seeing some blessing, but he lacked any perception of judgment that came with the great day of the Lord in the arrival of the kingdom of God. So he wondered, *Is this in fact the One we have been waiting for because only half of the equation is present?* There is blessing, but there is no judgment that would signify the consummation of the arrival of the kingdom of God.

I would submit to you that that same distortion, or that same misunderstanding, is present today. People assume that since the judgment has not occurred, therefore the kingdom of God has not arrived. But didn't Jesus answer that very question that John the Baptist himself posed? So, on the one hand, if John the Baptist was confused, I suppose we could say that if we're confused, we're in good company. But on the other hand, Jesus supplied an answer that reassured John. Shouldn't we also be reassured by the same answer?

In reply, Jesus quotes Old Testament prophesy to John about healing the blind, about causing the lame to walk. He showed what his words and works made clear, that John was right to look for both blessing and judgment, but wrong to seek both at once. Jesus told him that the kingdom comes in two phases, and that blessing will precede judgment. John announced that the hope of God's visitation was soon to come, and Jesus announced that the hope was being fulfilled. Jesus did also speak of a coming judgment at some length in Matthew 24 and in the parallel gospels. He warned that not one stone would be left upon another in the Temple. He told them that in the world there would be tribulations, there would be false prophets, false christs, and signs from heaven, and that all this would occur before even that generation had passed.

In Matthew 16:28: "There are some standing here who will not taste death until they see the Son of Man coming in His kingdom." Those who would advocate a kingdom still far off, even if only as future as tomorrow, struggle with this verse, for Jesus here says there are some who are alive now who will not die until they see the kingdom of God . . ."the Son of Man coming in His kingdom." The destruction of Jerusalem in AD 70 is described as but the beginning of birth pangs for the gospel to be proclaimed throughout the whole earth—the beginning of birth pangs, not the end of all things.

Out of the destruction of Jerusalem, the Church is born. With Jerusalem and all Old Testament understanding then pressed aside—not the covenants and not the promises of the Old Testament, but the Old Testament misconceptions and the trusting in the types and the shadows rather than the reality—all that now being set aside; the spiritual life of the Church of Christ begins to emerge around the world. With the destruction of the Temple, the kingdom can be rightly said to have come.

First Corinthians 3:16 and 17 speak of the Church, saying that she is God's temple, and God's Spirit dwells in her. She, the Church, this Bride of Christ, the one Christ himself has established is the temple of the holy God, and there is where he dwells. Why does he dwell there? Because there we find the expression of his kingdom. Jesus was ushering in the kingdom of God in words and deeds and miracles and preaching. The kingdom is so connected with the Person of Jesus that Philip even equated the two in Acts 8:12 when it says "They believed Philip as he preached the good news about the kingdom of God and the name of Jesus."

To preach the kingdom of God is to preach Christ. We can't separate the two. The kingdom itself is found in the Person of Christ, and the Spirit of Christ dwells in his people. This helps us understand Jesus' teaching to the Pharisees when they asked him when the kingdom would come. That was what they wanted to know. When will the kingdom come? That seems to be a question that even extends in the debate up to our very day. When is this kingdom going to come? And again, Jesus answers in Luke 17, verses 20 and 21. "The kingdom of God is not coming with signs to be observed, nor will they say, 'Look, here it is!' or 'There!' for behold, the kingdom of God is in the midst of you." In his very Person, the kingdom of God was present.

What does this mean to us? What does this mean to all men? Not only did Jesus bring the kingdom, but he embodies the kingdom. There is no kingdom to be discovered outside of the Person of Jesus Christ. So if there is going to be a Temple that is rebuilt in an effort to bring in the kingdom of God, that Temple has been replaced by Christ. What else did he say when he said, "Tear this Temple down, and in three days I will build it up again?" He was speaking of his own Person, and yet well-intentioned Christians even today will raise funds and will seek for the rebuilding of the Temple, which in the sovereign rule of God was destroyed.

What are the evidences that the kingdom of God is present? We may have a phrase or a teaching here or there, but can we say there is evidence that the kingdom of God is actually present? Yes. The Scripture gives us abundant evidence of the kingdom of God being present. First and foremost, we would point to the defeat of Satan. Matthew 12:28 and Luke 11:20, record the great change in the spiritual realm in which we are made to dwell. Jesus said, "But if it is by the finger of God that I cast out demons, then the kingdom of God has come upon you." Jesus was there saying that his power and authority to cast demons out, to have rule over demons, demonstrates that the power of God, and the kingdom of God has now come to displace the kingdom and the rule of Satan.

When the 72 returned from their preaching journey, Jesus said to them that he "saw Satan fall like lightning from heaven." This complements the binding of Satan that is described in Revelation, chapter 20, this binding of Satan that comes with the kingdom of God. Jesus said, "I saw him fall like lightning as you were out preaching the kingdom." The coming of the kingdom means that Christ has broken the yoke of Satan's oppressive rule over God's people. And through death, Jesus has rendered him powerless who had the power of death, that is the devil. And by his resurrection, Jesus swallowed up death in victory and removed death's sting.

A second evidence besides the defeat of Satan is that Jesus worked miracles. Now often Jesus worked miracles that parallel his preaching of the kingdom. Herman Ridderbos, who has written a great deal about the kingdom of God, said that "Jesus preaches the kingdom with words and deeds."[2] Now disease is an effect of the fall and disease is an effect of Satan's dominion. In fact, when Scripture talks about those who were possessed by demons, weren't they very often diseased-ridden people? And then they were cleansed not only by the evacuation of the demon, but in their bodies as well.

---

2. Ridderbos, *The Gospel According to John*, 144.

The effect of the fall of Satan's dominion meant that the healing of sicknesses and the casting out of demons are sure signs of the kingdom's arrival. Consider what these healings would point to. When Jesus healed the blind, he often accompanied with the healing a teaching on the eyes of faith. When He healed the crippled, didn't he mention also the walking in righteousness? With the healing of the deaf, wasn't there implied a hearing and an understanding? When the lepers were cleansed, weren't they cleansed of sin and shame, in our understanding? And when the dead are raised, don't we understand being raised to a new life in Christ? Even the miracles themselves pointed to the realities of the perfect establishment of the kingdom of God, most particularly in the raising of Lazarus because it is the deliverance from the death that the kingdom is most distinguished as being present.

And thirdly, the preaching of the gospel itself. When John asked Jesus if he were the One and referred to his miracles, Jesus also referred to the preaching of the gospel. What the Old Testament prophets foretold and the law shadowed, Jesus preached as having arrived in the gospel. Jesus taught as One having authority, and his teaching continually amazed them.

Fourth, there is the reality of salvation. Many times in the gospels, salvation is described as entering into the kingdom of God. For example, in Matthew 5:20, "For I tell you, unless your righteousness exceeds that of the scribes and Pharisees, you will never enter the kingdom of heaven." Matthew 18:3: "Truly, I say to you, unless you turn and become like children, you will never enter the kingdom of heaven." In Mark 9:47: "And if your eye causes you to sin, tear it out. It is better for you to enter the kingdom of God with one eye than with two eyes to be thrown into hell." The kingdom is present because Jesus forgave and forgives sins. And in that forgiveness is salvation, and salvation can also be described as entering into the kingdom of God.

And then fifth and finally, it is a spiritual kingdom. When the Pharisees asked when the kingdom was coming, Jesus said that it doesn't come with careful observation because it is in within you. And when Pilate asked about the kingdom, Jesus said, "My kingdom is not of this world." Jesus' kingdom is very real in the spiritual domain, and we who are living spirits are in it, just as Jesus told his disciples in Mark 9:1. "There are some standing here who will not taste death until they see the kingdom of God after it has come with power."

Let's summarize and draw a couple of conclusions. First of all, we've established the kingdom of God arrived in the Person of Jesus, and that it is spiritual, and that there were many evidences of several different types to prove it. While we didn't explore in any depth the notion of a thousand-year future reign, we can be comfortable accepting that the thousand years of Revelation 20 begin with the binding of Satan, and that is already accomplished by Christ, and stands for an indefinite period of time in which Christ rules, if in fact he is ruling in a kingdom now, which he is.

Secondly, we can find guidance for our own living from the prayer we so frequently recite in the words, "Thy kingdom come, Thy will be done in earth, as it is in heaven." To know God's will is to know how to live, for God's will is perfect and unchanging. As we read in Malachi, God said, "It is not I who has changed. It's not I who has forgotten anything. It's you who have been unfaithful to my will." As people of the kingdom, we are to live lives that are transformed by the gospel that has announced the kingdom's arrival.

In every letter, and in many of the gospels, from the Beatitudes to the Fruit of the Spirit, the distinguished ethic of a Christian is described. It's not left to wonder what God's will is for us. It's left for us to read and to be transformed. This ethic doesn't earn or add to salvation, of course, because salvation is a gift from our King. But the Christian ethic does reflect God's rule on earth as it is in heaven.

So what difference does it make whether the kingdom is present now or coming later? Do you want Satan defeated now or later? You want him bound now or later? You want the Restrainer to be in place now or later? Do you want death and grave destroyed now, or are you okay with leaving that until later? Do you want the gift of life in your spirit now, or are you willing to hold off with a promissory note for that to be accomplished sometime later? Will you plan to be living as a citizen in Christ's kingdom now, recognizing his lordship now, or do you plan to begin to be obedient to the Lord later?

9

An Un-comprehended Truth

John 18:37–38

> Then Pilate said to him, "So you are a king?'" Jesus answered, "You say that I am a king. For this purpose I was born and for this purpose I have come into the world— to bear witness to the truth. Everyone who is of the truth listens to my voice." Pilate said to Him, "What is truth?"

I remind you, we are still examining the appearance of Christ before Pilate in a time of the trial of Christ before his crucifixion.

John 8:32 promises us, "You will know the truth, and the truth will set you free." What is truth? C. S. Lewis, in his book *God and the Dock*, wrote, "Truth is always about something, but reality is that about which truth is."[1] Men are forever working to figure out just how to parse truth. Richard Allen, who was the National Security Advisor to President Reagan, once received a thousand dollars in cash and two watches from a Japanese journalist who wanted to thank him for arranging an interview with Nancy Reagan. When asked upon the reception of this gift, Richard Allen said, "I didn't accept it; I just received it." Margaret Thatcher said, "You don't tell deliberate lies, but sometimes you have to be evasive."[2]

When we talk about truth, we recognize that more often than not people excuse themselves as not being liars when they just tell half truths or white lies, which is somehow less than, I suppose, a lie of another color. Deceptions are employed in all sorts of conversations, covering everything from the trivial to the questions of life and death. Kids lie about

---

1. Martindale. *The Quotable C.S. Lewis,* 588.
2. Thatcher, *American Reference Books,* 25.

their homework. Courts lie about when life begins. In religion, truth has also become a casualty in a quest for spiritual significance. People say things like, "It's true for you, but not for me." Or, "That's how you see it. That's not how I see it," as if language can no longer carry truth in the words that are read or expressed.

True for you but not for me has become more than a slogan; it's become a way of faith. But truth, real truth, cannot be fragmented because truth is unity. You cannot take truth and piecemeal it out, and pick and choose the truths you want because truth is embodied in a Person, and that Person is Christ. All truth is God's truth.

For example, there was a time when the Church said the earth had to be the center of the universe, and that all things, including the sun, had to orbit around the earth. When the truth became known because of the advances of science, the Church resisted accepting truth and said that all theology would fly apart, as if the truth were not whole. But Colossians 1:17 was proved when it said, it is by Christ that all things exist. When eventually science is able to dig deep enough and to show it, it will not disprove this verse. It will show that even the atom is held together because of the Lord Jesus Christ in whom God has embodied all truth. How will that be? We don't have the answer yet, but so far, science has done nothing to prove that anything in the Scriptures is not true.

"Everyone may be entitled to his or her own opinion," says Doug Groothuis, "but everyone is not entitled to their own truth because truth is but one." In *Preaching to a Postmodern World*, a book by Graham Johnston, he wrote, "Today post-modernity says you can only believe what's in your own heart. Count on intuition and faith. Give up on the idea of truth. Have an experience instead."[3] In light of this spirit of postmodern relativism, Pontius Pilate could be considered to have a very modern way of thinking.

Who is Pontius Pilate? Have you ever pondered this one who made such a serious inquiry of the Lord, one who is given such space in the Scripture and yet is not a Jew nor even a gentile believer? We're given the details of the conversation in the Scriptures, but who was this man Pontius Pilate? Where did this question concerning truth come from in his own life? Was it purely random? Is he a fictitious character just deposited in the Scriptures to act as a foil for Christ?

---

3. Johnston, *Preaching to a Postmodern World*, 9.

No, Pontius Pilate was very real. In correspondence to his friend Caligula, King Herod Agrippa described Pontius Pilate as, "A man of an unbending and ruthlessly hard character." In his time, corruption, violence, robbery, oppression, humiliations, constant executions without trial, and unlimited, intolerable cruelty were the order of the day in Judea.

Now Herod Agrippa may have chosen to accentuate the negative. Other historical sources agree however that Pilate wasn't a man of noble character. Pilate arrived in Judea around 26 AD. He served as procurator for 10 years. There is no way he would have been left as procurator for 10 years unless he had been an able man—able in the sense of keeping the Jews settled and keeping them out of rebellion.

Prior to Pilate's arrival, the ones who had preceded him had always been careful not to offend the Jews' sensibilities. For example, they wouldn't carry banners into Jerusalem that had likenesses of the emperor on them. But when Pilate came to town, he saw that as a sign of weakness, and he in the middle of the night marched the troops in and posted the banners with the emperor's likeness on them. For five days straight after that, the Jews gathered in his courts and stood in front of his palace there protesting and calling out to him.

On the sixth day, he ordered them to appear at the hippodrome where he gathered his soldiers around them with their swords drawn as if to kill them. He told them that if they did not cease immediately, he in fact would order the Roman soldiers to kill them. The Jews' response was to immediately, all of them to a man, fall on their face and bare their necks. Pilate was taken aback by this expression of devotion; he relented, and removed the banners.

Philo and Josephus, great historians, agree with many other historical records that detail the cruel deeds of Pilate. So why do we have a picture in the gospels of a man seeking to understand, seeking to actually save Christ as One in whom he could find no guilt, from the Jews who were after the blood of our Lord?

The answer can be found in the fact that Pilate simply despised the Jews, and he took every opportunity to let them know it. His disposition was one of opposition when he received this dubious request to condemn. He understood they weren't coming because they respected his judgment. They were coming because they wanted to accomplish something that only he could accomplish. They wanted to use him to carry out an execution of a Man whom they didn't like. He knew them well enough to know that they sought to use him and rid themselves of someone they despised, and so his resistance was even greater after he spoke to Jesus and found that he was clearly no political threat.

Pilate had asked Jesus whether he was a king. Jesus didn't deny he was a king because Jesus speaks the truth. But he did say the character and nature of his kingdom was not one that was interested in occupying Pilate's own palace, that it was not one interested in geography or conquest. It was not one interested in armies and swords. It was of a completely different nature. It was one that was born in truth. It was born, in Pilate's view, in the world of philosophical inquiry. And philosophical inquiry was something that the Romans understood quite well.

Jesus' dominion was not over bodies, but over minds and souls. He conquered not by violence, but by persuasion of the truth. Pilate understood politics, and he understood power grabs, but truth? Truth? Is that what this is all about? Ideas? From Pilate's perspective, this was a duel between the truth of the Pharisees, religious traditions, and the ideas of this revolutionary religious teacher. Pilate's background grew out of that Greek philosophy which had not yet answered the question of man's purpose. Though philosophers like Plato had committed their entire lives nobly to seeking an answer to this one great question, Pilate knew that for all the years of inquiry and thought and schools given solely to answer this question, the answer yet evaded them.

So now he looked down at this poor Galilean. Compared to the Aristotles and the Platos of the past, was this anonymous figure, this uneducated Man with a very small following of disciples, now going to tell him truth, where Aristotle and Plato had failed? He looked at this beaten, arrested Galilean with a death sentence hanging over his head, and this Galilean was going to tell him what truth was. Pilate would have been very pressed to take him seriously.

He was a cynical man, committed to Epicurean living, for what else could satisfy him in life? These are echoes of Frederick Nietzsche's quote, "There are no eternal facts as there are no absolute truths." This would have been Pilate's perspective. There had been nothing absolute that had been proven in Greek philosophy. Christ was talking about nothing of the sort. Nothing that would have resulted in a new kingdom and a new way of life that would have displaced Rome. Considering the work of Plato and the Stoics and so many other great thinkers, what was Pilate to think about when he looked at this beaten, poor Galilean in Jerusalem of all places? And now he was hearing a claim to know truth? Now we can see why he would turn away muttering a question that carries weight to this day, "What is truth?"

"What is truth?" remains a question even today. We can see in Pilate the cynicism and the dissatisfaction and the distrust of an entire world, which even today when the Church says, "We know the truth," is turned to a cynical, "But what is truth?" Truth is the characteristic of Christ's kingdom. His kingship is over all that is true. What is true is what is real, and what is true holds all things together, and it springs from his very purpose.

In Pilate's world, Rome ruled by power without regard to man's principles or convictions or morality. Rome was a kingdom that threw away any who could not serve, but kept those who would pay taxes and entered them into the rolls of citizen—a very pragmatic approach to kingdom and government. But if a person will be a citizen in the kingdom of Christ, it is not their tax paying ability which is sought, but their heart. It is their life which is to be considered. Those whose lives issue from truth hear the voice of their true King.

Sir Arthur Conan Doyle said, "When you have eliminated the impossible, whatever remains, however improbable, must be the truth."[4] What an interesting default position to take, to say that we will discover truth by eliminating everything that is untrue. Christ is saying, "I am the source of truth." It ends all confusion and all debate because God who is the Creator has established everything from physical laws to the morality of man. He has created us in his own image. Where else will we find a source or a wellspring of anything that is true except in the mind and in the action of our Creator?

Jesus of Nazareth had introduced Pilate to the kingdom and to his own purpose which was to testify to that kingdom whose chief characteristic is truth. Pilate knew the charges against Jesus were without substance, and yet there was something about Jesus that so threatened religious Israel that they were begging Rome to kill him, and that intrigued Pilate. He saw before him a Man whom he would count nothing more than a beggar, a vagabond, a nameless, faceless, anonymous Jew. But while this Man was no threat to Rome, something about his teaching had so incited the Jews that they wanted him destroyed. Something about the way Jesus

---

4. Doyle, *Bartlett's Familiar Quotations*, 577.

delivered the Word of God incensed the Jews such that they couldn't allow for him just to continue to teach. He had to be destroyed. And that puzzled Pilate.

The truth that evaded Pilate was of a kingdom that he couldn't conceive because although Christ's kingdom was arriving right in front of him, he had no ability to recognize it. I like Donald Grey Barnhouse's emphasis on the word *kingship* rather than kingdom because kingdom in our understanding has to do with a place. It has to do more with a physical structure or even with laws. But kingship is the dominion of a king, the right to rule. And that really is more what Jesus is expressing, isn't it? The kingship of the kingdom of God.

"For this cause," Jesus said, "for this very reason I came." We were brought into this world, but Jesus came. He has described himself in this way on several occasions. In Luke, chapter 19, the 10th verse: "For the Son of Man came to seek and to save the lost." Mark, chapter 2, verse 17: "I came not to call the righteous, but sinners." Or Mark, chapter 10:45: "For even the Son of Man came not to be served but to serve, and to give his life as a ransom for many."

You may believe we're making much of nothing by saying, "Well, he came," or "He was sent," whichever it might be, but the Scriptures are quite clear that the Spirit is *sent*; Christ *came*. In Philippians, chapter 2, when it talks about the humility of Christ, it said that though he had every right to every privilege that belonged to God, he himself made himself as nothing and came in the form of a servant. When we read about his second coming, we hear of the Son of Man who is coming down to judge. Thus the intention of Jesus in coming to establish his kingdom needs to be remembered.

By his question, Pilate shows that he puts Jesus outside the realm of those who are to be taken seriously. "What is truth?" he says as he disregards any thought of listening to Jesus' response. The battle between flesh and spirit raged in the trials of Jesus, and it raged in the person of Pilate. Jesus explained to him because Pilate asked clearly, "Are you a king?" Jesus, who would not deny his own kingship, explained to Pilate the nature of the kingdom; however, the spirit failed, and the flesh prevailed.

In that question, "Is there a truth?" Pilate proved he was alien to the Person and life of Christ and to the kingdom now before him, and he could hear only with ears. He heard the words because he echoed them in his question, but he heard with ear, not with the heart.

Pilate's question is a modern question. It's modern because his question begins from a position of disbelief. It's modern because it begins without comprehension. He could not understand what Jesus was saying, and his question comes from that lack of understanding. It's a modern question because it's cynical, and it's rhetorical. He didn't wait for a response. He didn't expect a response. I would even dare say he would not have wanted or even accepted a response. He turned, and he left.

What is truth? Think of the moment of opportunity in this man's life. He had before him the Lord of lords. He had before him God incarnate, in the flesh, who said, "I came to tell you about the truth." And he asks the right question, "Then what is the truth?" but he asked it with his back turned. How often has the world done the same thing? They say, "Well, what does Christianity have to say about that?" and they do so as they're turning to walk the other way. They don't really care to hear what Christianity has to say about anything. They simply want to do the service of saying we gave them a chance to respond.

If the question is modern, then so is the presentation of the kingdom that prompted the question. Jesus has called himself the Spirit and the Scripture truth. He has told Pilate he came to bear testimony to the truth of these three things. Jesus has called himself the way, the truth, and the life. He has called the Spirit the Spirit of truth. And he has called the Scriptures that were written also true. All truth as described by Jesus comes from above. Jesus by the immaculate conception and the incarnation, the Holy Spirit by the procession and indwelling in man, the Scriptures by inspiration all bear testimony to the truth.

God has not left us without a source of truth. He has not left us to wonder. He has not left us to doubt. He has given us truth. All truth in the world is not written specifically in the pages of Scripture, but Scripture certainly limits all that is in the world whether or not it is true. All science properly ultimately proves truth. It has never yet disproven it. There are theories that abound, and theories are often accepted as truth even if unproven, but once proven, the theory either fails, or it proves out what God has decreed.

The kingdom which is born in truth exists in the Person of Christ. Pilate was looking for some abstract, philosophical truth, but truth is found in the Person of Christ, the embodiment of truth. Everything he touched, everything he said, everything he did, most importantly the redemption of man and the reconciliation of man to our Father at the

Cross, and then being the first fruits of the resurrection, the promise and the seal of that which is to come, all of this bears testimony to truth.

What is the answer to his question? You know what it is. He asked, "What is truth?" Jesus said, "I am the way, and the truth, and the life." He is the One who has answered the question of man's purpose. He is the One who is revealing all spiritual mystery. He is the One in whom salvation and the kingdom is found. What is truth? We all can answer that question.

10

Not This Man But Barabbas

John 18:38b-40

> After he had said this, he went back outside to the Jews and told them, "I find no guilt in him. But you have a custom that I should release one man for you at the Passover. So do you want me to release to you the King of the Jews?" They cried out again, "Not this man, but Barabbas!" Now Barabbas was a robber.

The Gospels—Matthew, Mark, Luke, and John—all relate the life and ministry of Christ. All are inspired by God. Each is written in a style unique to the apostles from whose pen the story is told. In many cases, a particular event or miracle is captured. Sometimes it is related in great detail, and in other times you find in another gospel that the event or ministry is completely omitted. We might be told by one apostle of a particular event, and then not told by another. John acknowledges as much in chapter 20, verse 30, when he writes, "Now Jesus did many other signs in the presence of the disciples, which are not written in this book." So John tells us that Jesus did many more things than he was able to record in his own book. But taken together, the four gospels weave for us a rich tapestry and present a well-rounded and multi-dimensional portrait of the Savior's life.

When we find an event in the gospels that is addressed in all four, we need to take note. In the case of the story of Barabbas, John is actually one of the more brief accounts, briefer than any of the other three accounts which we find in the Scriptures. There are a total of 38 verses used to tell the story of Barabbas. That's more than the space that the Scriptures use to relate the story of Judas' betrayal. John takes only about three verses to give us the basic account of Barabbas. The other gospels give us a more expanded explanation.

The outline of the story of Barabbas seems simple enough. In verse 38, Pilate announced to the Jews that he had concluded his inquiry of Jesus' case, and he judged that Jesus was innocent. He found no fault in this Man. In Matthew, Mark, and especially Luke, the roar of the crowd's accusation is mentioned. Jesus' silence before the crowds emboldened Pilate even more concerning Jesus' innocence. The crowd began to roar, as it's related in the other accounts. Pilate, we must imagine, looked over at Jesus, expecting Jesus to protest or to proclaim his own innocence. Jesus remained silent before the crowd which was calling for his crucifixion, and Pilate marveled at that and became even more convinced of his innocence.

In verse 39, the curious event occurs. Having found no guilt in Jesus, we would expect Pilate in a stroke of justice to release Jesus. He had already proclaimed that he found no fault. But instead, he seemed to ignore his own judgment, and he presented it to the mob as a way more of advice than of judgment. Even though Jesus was innocent, he turned to the gathered mob—and I use that word on purpose because they were acting like a mob—and he seemed to be asking what he should do. "I find him to be innocent, but what do you think we ought to do?" Clearly, the whole situation, from the concerns of his wife who had a disturbing dream about Jesus, perhaps his own animosity towards the Jews, and then his conversation with Jesus seem to have put Pilate off balance. He was not sure what he should do about Jesus.

We gather from the other gospels that at this point Pilate heard the Sanhedrin expanding their charge of sedition to the time when Jesus lived in Galilee. They were saying, "Even when he was in Galilee, right up to the time now in Jerusalem, he has been seditious, and he has been a criminal against the state, and no friend of Caesar." Pilate seized on the opportunity, and he sent Jesus to Herod when he heard that Jesus was in Galilee, but nothing was accomplished with Herod except that he donated an old, purple robe. And he put it on Jesus and sent him back.

Again Pilate affirmed that he saw no reason for condemnation. He found no reason to sentence Jesus to die. He was torn between his own misgivings over the injustice that was being done to Jesus and some sort of a fear of Jewish complaint to Rome, or perhaps some mob action and insurrection. By the time Jesus returned to Pilate from Herod, a crowd had begun to gather in the court, and it was there that Pilate now found himself.

He sought an escape through custom and tradition, through consensus opinion. Maybe he expected some sympathy with the mob when he asked the question that would somehow help bolster his position against the will of the Sanhedrin. He had to be aware that only five days before Jesus had entered to great accolades and a great reception at the triumphal entry. He had to know that there was some popularity with Jesus among the people. So perhaps when he asked the question, he thought the mob would simply affirm his own testimony concerning Christ, and that that would isolate the Sanhedrin, and that he would be able to push his way on forward through the Sanhedrin. But instead he found the mob to be influenced more by the Sanhedrin.

In verse 40, the mob returned their verdict. "Do not release the innocent man, but release the robber Barabbas." By *robber*, we know that Barabbas was an insurrectionist, and according to the expanded accounts in the other gospels, even a murderer. Insurrection was the very crime Jesus was being accused of! Here his innocence had been proclaimed after he had been judged, and a real insurrectionist would be released while the innocent Man would be killed instead.

This reveals the true concern of the religious party. They came, saying, "We're concerned because this man Jesus is going to cause the people to have an insurrection, which then will bring Rome down upon us, and overthrow our rule, and put Jerusalem into captivity." Recall for a moment, in an earlier chapter, we discussed the great privileges which Rome had granted to the Jews. They were even excused from military service, they were allowed to conduct their own worship, and they were not required to bend a knee to the gods of Rome, or to pay homage to Caesar. These were great privileges. The Sanhedrin was allowed to make judgments and rulings all the way up to, but not including, the death penalty.

They were concerned, they said, that they would lose these things if Jesus, the great insurrectionist, were allowed to go free. But then they called for an actual insurrectionist, one who had already proved he was an insurrectionist, one who had actually been condemned for murder. They asked for him to be released because Jesus' threat to them was not through Rome, but through the Spirit.

The Sanhedrin here proved conclusively that they were a people under tremendous conviction from the teaching of Jesus. They recognized the truth of his teaching. They had no answer to his teaching, and they wanted him destroyed. They wanted him gone, even if it meant the release of one who actually was guilty.

Friedrich Krummacher commented on the present implications from the verdict of this Jewish mob in his book titled simply *The Suffering Savior*. He said, "More than an echo of this cry resounds through the world to this day for all who reject Christ as the Savior of sinners and are eager on the contrary for the upholding of the honor, independence, and liberty of their old man."[1]

In Barabbas, we see the great exchange. We see what is formally called *vicarious atonement*. An innocent man condemned; a guilty man set free. A rejection of Jesus is a decision to remain unmoved in a cell where we have been condemned to die for our own sin. James Montgomery Boice, speaking to this very same issue, elaborates on a similar point. He says, "The decision of the mob was the world's decision. The world will ever choose a robber, an insurrectionist, or murder to the guiltless Christ. Why? Because Barabbas was of the world, and is the world. Barabbas was one of them, and however dangerous he might have been, he was at least controllable. They could handle him, but how do you handle Jesus?"[2]

Let me try to synthesize these two perspectives into one thought because both of them are true, and both need to be kept in mind when we hear the words, "Free Barabbas." One of the saddest narratives in the gospels is that of the rich, young ruler. In that story, a rich, young ruler comes to Jesus, and he asks what he can do to guarantee his eternal life. His tone is respectful, his question is relevant, and he certainly has asked the one Person in all of history who can give him an accurate and right response.

Jesus tells him simply this—and I summarize the intent of what Jesus said—that this man was to divest himself of everything in life that gave him a sense first of all of his own self-righteousness, but more important than that even, self-sufficiency. And then he was to take his life, and he was to commit it to discipleship, living under the constant presence and direction of the Lord.

Obviously, the young man expected something a bit more manageable, something he could direct, something he could control, something

---

1. Krummacher, *The Suffering Savior*, 295
2. Boice, *The Gospel of John*, 1459.

he could opt in or opt out of, something he could do partially, something he could simply set aside if the calling of Christ should interfere with his own desires and ambitions. In the end, he left, returning to the life that he knew and was comfortable with.

This is applicable to the poor man as well as to the rich. It's applicable to the young and the old. Can a leopard change his own spots? In the end, we are told, a dog will always return to its own vomit.

Pilate asked the people, "What shall I do with Jesus?" And as if bearing testimony to their understanding of the teaching of Christ, they demanded the Light be removed from their darkness. Take the Light away. Too much of Jesus, too much light, too much preaching of the gospel, too much ministry of the Church, too much commitment being called upon, too much surrender of our own lives to Christ. You're asking too much. Take it away. Matthew explains that they asked for Pilate to, in the words of the original, *apollesosin*, that is, destroy Jesus. They asked Pilate to destroy Jesus. How deep the hatred ran for the One who brought the gospel.

But what of Barabbas himself? What of this man who was to be released? While Hollywood likes to show us Barabbas standing by Jesus there at the top of the stairs with Pilate, the gospels do not give us an account anywhere that Barabbas was actually present when the mob is shouting. He most likely was still sitting in his cell, a place of darkness, a place without any hope of release. Every footstep Barabbas would hear coming down the corridor, he would most likely imagine was the executioner on the way to take him to his own death.

But this time, when he heard the footsteps, and he heard the sliding of the bolt on his door as the door was swung open, he received word, not that he was on his way to his own execution, but that he had been spared. He had been released. He was not going to trial. His record was cleared, and he was a free man. The people had decided instead to destroy an innocent and a righteous man so that the guilty man may be set free.

The man who brings Barabbas this news is parallel to our own evangelist, isn't he? The story he brings Barabbas is that this One they call Jesus, he will die instead of you. This One they call Jesus is innocent, but he will stand in your place, and he will die while you are set free. We are burdened with sin and guilt. In fact, because of our own treason against God, our own insurrections against the Lord and his kingdom, here in his own Church, we ourselves could be under the very same sentence of death. But then we are told of a glorious exchange—his life for ours. The Righteous for the sinner.

Krummacher eloquently states the implications of this. "After Christ has made the mysterious exchange with you, we are commissioned of God to inform you in plain terms that from the moment in which the holy Jesus took your place, you assumed his, and are installed into all the rights and immunities of the citizens of the kingdom."[3] This is the justification that comes by faith—justification, in that no sin will be laid at our feet. We are the ones who are counted as righteous even as he took our place as the unrighteous. He was not prosecuted or condemned for any sin of his own, but for our own sin which is placed upon him even as his righteousness is placed upon us in that great exchange of vicarious atonement. Any who are in Christ, we're told, have been judged already. It's by faith that those, and only those, who have heard the voice of the Savior and believed will be sprung from their dungeons and their cells.

So many of the hymns which form the prayers and the confessions of faith of the Church have been shaped with this idea in mind, this vicarious, substitutive atonement of Christ. That is what we mean when we say that Jesus died in our place. The hymn *Amazing Grace* trumpets God's salvation of a blind and pitiful wretch who deserves nothing but condemnation. Charles Wesley's great hymn *And Can It Be?* puts the issue before us plainly.

> Long my imprisoned spirit lay,
> Fast bound in sin and nature's night;
> Thine eye diffused a quickening ray-
> I woke, the dungeon flamed with light;
> My chains fell off, my heart was free,
> I rose, went forth, and followed Thee.
> My chains fell off, my heart was free,
> I rose, went forth, and followed Thee.

Isn't our experience much like that of Barabbas? We've lived in rebellion against the holy government of God, and yet God comes and releases us from our dungeon where we are condemned, under sentence of death, for high treason against the Creator.

H. A. Ironside tells a story. It's a wonderful story of a Jewish man and his friend who was a Christian. They were very close, and they frequently

---

3. Krummacher, *The Suffering Savior*, 233.

ate lunch together. The Christian often would tell the Jewish man his faith, desperately desiring that the Jewish man would come to faith. There was never really any response by him. He politely listened to his friend as he continued to tell him of his Christian belief and faith. He listened, and he listened, and he listened.

One day, a great sickness fell upon the Jewish man. His Christian friend sought to see him but was told that because of his condition he would not be able to see him. Finally, at the very end, he was allowed to come in. He knelt in prayer beside his friend's bed. He took his hand which had already grown very thin and was so weak he could hardly grip at all. He continued to pray, and he prayed aloud that God would save him and that Christ would visit himself upon his heart. His Jewish friend's eyes cracked open, and his head turned over to him, and his lips began to move, and all he said before he passed was this, "Not Barabbas, but this man."

Have you languished in dungeons of disbelief yourself? Are you still bound by that which you found empowered to control in your own life? Is religion just fine as long as it can be tamed, and it's on your schedule, and it's according to the way you want it to be? As long as you can shape it the way you think it ought to be? As long as it appeals to your sensitivities and suits you in your preferences and the things you like to do? Is that how you like to craft your own church in a community? Are you still bound by those things that you alone are able to control?

"What would you have me do with Jesus?" Pilate says. What would you have me do with Jesus? Will you receive him for whom he claims to be? Will you at last be set free, Barabbas?

11

He Suffered Under Pontius Pilate

John 19:4–16

Pilate went out again and said to them, "See, I am bringing him out to you that you may know that I find no guilt in him." So Jesus came out, wearing the crown of thorns and the purple robe. Pilate said to them, "Behold the man!" When the chief priests and the officers saw him, they cried out, "Crucify him, crucify him!" Pilate said to them, "Take him yourselves and crucify him, for I find no guilt in him." The Jews answered him, "We have a law, and according to that law he ought to die because he has made himself the Son of God."

When Pilate heard this statement, he was even more afraid. He entered his headquarters again and said to Jesus, "Where are you from?" But Jesus gave him no answer. So Pilate said to him, "You will not speak to me? Do you not know that I have authority to release you and authority to crucify you?" Jesus answered him, "You would have no authority over me at all unless it had been given you from above. Therefore he who delivered me over to you has the greater sin."

From then on Pilate sought to release him, but the Jews cried out, "If you release this man, you are not Caesar's friend. Everyone who makes himself a king opposes Caesar." So when Pilate heard these words, he brought Jesus out and sat down on the judgment seat at a place called The Stone Pavement, and in Aramaic Gabbatha. Now it was the day of Preparation of the Passover. It was about the sixth hour. He said to the Jews, "Behold your King!" They cried out, "Away with him, away with him, crucify him!" Pilate said to them, "Shall I crucify your King?" The chief priests answered, "We have no king but Caesar." So he delivered him over to them to be crucified."

The passage presents us with the drama of Christ's passion. It is written not as merely a didactic account but rather in such vivid and active detail that it evokes an emotional response from us. We're made to see it, to hear it, to feel it, to enter into it. Don't keep it at a distance. Listen to the dialogue of our Lord with Pilate. Listen as Pilate ponders and wonders and puzzles over this Man before him. Enter into that dialogue. Enter into the voice of the crowd which calls out for his crucifixion. Don't keep it so far removed as to simply be a historical account of the last days of our Savior's life.

We've looked in some detail at the phases of the trial, Gethsemane, betrayal by Judas, Peter's denial. We've looked in some detail even at the scourging of Jesus. Let's quickly review the narrative of these last hours in the life of Jesus and frame the trials together for their conclusion, a verdict, and a sentence.

Peter Lange's homiletical outline of the trials is a wonderful summary of our Lord in the trials. He said, "Christ, at once being judged by and judging the world. Christ, at the bar of the Roman state, Christ before Pilate, and Pilate before Christ. How Christ's glance pierced through all the mazes of judgment, through all entanglements to the right, through all concealments and misrepresentations to the bottom, through all ambiguities to the purpose, through all waverings to the issue. How the judgment of the Lord judgeth itself in its accusations, in its examinations, and in the motives for its sentence."[1]

After the betrayal of Judas and arrest in Gethsemane, Jesus was taken to Annas where the Sanhedrin hoped to garner, or to begin to build a case against Jesus. Annas failed to deliver any help at all to the council against Jesus, and so Jesus was quickly taken from there to Caiaphas, who was the residing high priest, and to the Sanhedrin. Witnesses were paraded through with complaints ranging from self-contradictory issues to the ridiculous until one finally recounted the testimony of Jesus when he said that if they would tear down that Temple, he would build it again in three days.

Caiaphas became frustrated that Jesus wouldn't confirm or deny any charge that was made against him, and so he asked him outright whether he was the Christ, the Son of God. Jesus, at this point, not only affirmed the charge, but promised that the next time Caiaphas saw him, he will be

---

1. Lange, *A Commentary on the Holy Scriptures*, 573.

the Judge who standing over Caiaphas as the Son of Man. Caiaphas seized upon this, charged Jesus with blasphemy, and tore his robe. That verdict would require stoning according to Jewish custom and law, but they weren't allowed capital punishment under the yoke of Rome. Caiaphas was forced to turn to Rome and to Pontius Pilate, the procurator, for help.

Pontius Pilate himself was a creature of politics. Of above-average intelligence, he sought his own advancement, and he held the Jews with nothing but the deepest contempt. He was in Jerusalem because of the constant concern of revolt against the empire whenever the Jews gathered for feasts. The Sanhedrin approached Pilate and nuanced the charge a bit from a crime against God to a crime against the kingdom.

Remember that it was the zealots of Jesus' generation who would in a few short years to follow, AD 70, finally get enough traction and finally win enough hearts in their cry, "No king but God" to cause an outright rebellion against Rome, which would result in that insurrection with the actual destruction of Jerusalem and the Temple. So the atmosphere at the time when Jesus was brought in to Pilate was one in which Pilate was well aware of the activity of the zealots, thankful that so few were willing to give them any credence and actually rise up and revolt, but still wary because there was a definite threat of discontent and rebellion among the people. Days not unlike the days in which we find ourselves.

Pilate begrudgingly received Jesus for an interview. He really would have preferred to have nothing to do with this from the very beginning. This was Jewish business. But nevertheless, trying to keep the peace, ever the politician, he interviewed Christ. He found no crime in Jesus' conduct, but he struggled with the nature of the charge, that is until he heard the word *Galilee*. Ah! Jesus was a Galilean. That meant he was a subject of Herod, who was the son of Herod the Great—Herod the Great, who was infamous because of his command to destroy all of the children in Bethlehem.

Thus Jesus was sent to Herod, the son of Herod the Great. There Jesus was mocked in Herod's court, clothed with a purple robe, until finally Herod sends Jesus back, himself finding no reason for charge and without a verdict. Ralph Gorman sums up the situation well when he says, "Pilate found it difficult to get the affair off dead center. The Sanhedrinists accused Jesus, Pilate disbelieved their charges, and Jesus remained silent."[2]

In Luke 23:14 and 15, Pilate summed up the trial to the Sanhedrin. He told them that he had examined Jesus, and he had found nothing to charge him with. Herod also had examined him and found nothing worthy of charges. Pilate was seeking a way out, looking for some crack, some technicality or a legal loophole through which he could gracefully exit. Recognizing and remembering the great entry Jesus had into Jerusalem, which he surely would have received a report of, he knew Jesus was popular with the masses, and so he turned to the masses. He divested himself of responsibility for coming to a verdict and setting Christ free against the will of the Sanhedrin, and he turned to the masses presuming they were going to exonerate Jesus, thereby alleviating Pilate from this difficult position he was in. But unfortunately, the crowd that had been gathered there had already been swayed to the Sanhedrin view.

Pilate came out and reminded the people of the tradition by which one would be released during Passover; the people called for the zealot Barabbas who is in prison because of thievery and murder and insurrection. Pilate was still too much of a coward to set Jesus free, so he determined to have Jesus flogged hoping to satisfy the Sanhedrin's disdain for Christ. After the flogging, the soldiers, barely treating Jesus as a human being and actually even worse than they would treat their own beast, put a purple robe on him, and then they placed a crown of thorns on Him. Taking a reed which Jesus held in his hand, they begin to hit him in the head where the crown of thorns was located, driving the thorns deeper and deeper into his head. We don't know how long the soldiers had Jesus to their own abuse as they awaited Pilate's return, but the Scriptures seem to indicate that it was quite some time. Jesus, through all of this, suffered in silence.

Pilate ordered that Jesus be brought out again so that all could see the horrid condition of their Christ. Pilate still preferred to set Jesus free. He turned to the crowd, and he announced that he found no guilt in Jesus, and he ordered them to behold the Man, the famous words which have come down to us even in the Latin, *ecce homo*, behold the Man.

Gorman reflects on these words. "It would almost seem that Pilate, like Caiaphas, was used by God as an instrument of prophecy, and that

---

2. Gorman, *The Last Hours of Jesus*, 166.

his words go far beyond any meaning he intended they should have. It was almost as if he were saying to those present and to the generations yet to come, 'Behold the Man. Behold more than a Man. Behold him whose coming and whose present situation was foretold by the prophets, especially Isaiah. Behold him from whom alone comes the salvation of the world.' Again, we repeat in our own day, 'Behold the Man.'"[3]

It would seem that Pilate actually intended to appeal to the Jews' morality, to their sensitivities to the abuse of a man, by asking more or less how they could hope for any worse punishment on one of their own people at the hand of Rome. Or perhaps he was showing that this Man before them couldn't possibly be a threat to Rome. Look at him! Look at one of your own. Do you want any worse for one of your own at the hand of those who have the yoke of bondage over you? Look at this Man. Do you really take seriously any charge that he would be a threat to Caesar? He can do nothing. He is a beaten Man.

Whatever he hoped for, Pilate never imagined how dark and deep the hatred for Christ was in those who just wanted him dead. "I find no fault in him." Pilate confirmed the apostle Peter's words that Jesus was a Lamb without blemish and without spot. "I find no fault in this Man . . . this Lamb of God who has come to take away the sins of the world." Behold the Man! Behold the Lamb of God who comes to take away the sin of the world.

The answer to Pilate came quickly and clearly in one single word—*crucify*. Three times now Pilate had declared Jesus innocent. Three times he had declared there is no crime. His disgust at the Jews came out when he suggested that they do their own murdering and crucify Jesus themselves.

H. A. Ironside tells a remarkable story of a meeting of the synod of the Free Church of Scotland. A minister was asked to preach on Sunday morning on virtue, and as he was preaching, he gave a stirring message on virtue. His conclusion was, "O my friends, if virtue incarnate could only appear on earth, men would be so ravished by her beauty that they would fall down and worship her."

Everyone left that synod meeting remarking about how eloquent and how beautiful that sermon was. That same Sunday evening, a second minister came to deliver the evening message, preaching on the crucified

3. Ibid., 166.

Christ, and he concluded his sermon with these words, "My friends, virtue incarnate has appeared on earth, and men, instead of being ravished by his beauty and falling down and worshiping him, cried out, 'Away with him! Crucify him! Crucify him! We will not have this Man to reign over us.' That tells the wickedness of the natural heart, for those Jews that day were but representative men. They were not different men than any others, and no different than us." Then quoting from Romans 3:22–23, he read, "For there is no distinction: for all have sinned and fall short of the glory of God."[4] They, that is the Jews, tolled out the hatred of natural man to the holiness of God.

The Sanhedrin knew they were losing their case because each time Pilate came out, he declared he could find no reason to crucify this Man, Jesus. They were losing their case. They conferred. They made a quick decision. Jesus was no threat to Rome or Caesar. Fine then! They move off that, but as a good Roman, Pilate respects local law, and in John 19:7, the Sanhedrin disclosed finally the first nugget of truth that they have said all day—that Jesus declared himself to be the Son of God.

How ironic in the end that they showed their rejection of Jesus not with false charges, but by presenting him just as he presented himself to be. Their final rejection was not in trumping up a charge, or making anything up, or leaving any doubt that there was any misconception. They presented Jesus just as he has claimed himself to be, the Son of God. That was their final charge.

This new charge brought shocked silence from Pilate. He looked again to Jesus and was even more afraid. Up to now, he had been afraid of Caesar and Jewish politics, but now he was afraid of the nature of the Man who was standing before him. Pilate once again took Jesus aside.

Gorman has said, "Pilate had good reason to fear. He was a man of above-average intelligence and must have realized from the beginning of the trial that this man who stood before him was no ordinary prisoner cringing before his judge and multiplying answers to accusations. Jesus had remained as calm and silent as if another had been on trial. His patience and serenity, his disregard of the repeated charges of his enemies, his quiet majesty even when scourged and crowned with thorns and mocked as a royal pretender must have made a deep impression on Pilate.

---

4. Ironside, *Addresses on the Gospel of John*, 822.

And when he did speak, his words did nothing to allay Pilate's fears, for he said, 'My kingdom is not of this world.'"[5]

In pagan mythology, the idea of a god manifesting himself in human form was a real possibility. *Is Jesus some sort of greater king?* Pilate was asking himself. *Is he some sort of a god who has come down and appeared in flesh, who has a kingdom, and who has armies at his disposal?* Paganism allowed for these sorts of thoughts, just as it allows for many gods to have appeared on the stage of human history.

And so Pilate asked him a very plain question, one that sounds almost desperate, "Where are you from?" He knew Jesus hailed from Galilee, that he was called the Nazarene. None of this had been denied by Jesus. So what did Pilate want from Jesus now? "Are you from heaven, or are you from earth? Are you a god, or are you a man?" Again, Jesus remained silent.

Pilate then made a plea, almost sounding like he was Christ's own advocate. He reminded Jesus that all he had to do was say the word, and Jesus would go free. He wasn't asking for a sign, he wasn't asking for a miracle, he wasn't asking to be rewarded with a gift. He just wanted Jesus to tell him if he was in fact a god or a man. I'm convinced Pilate was both desperate to find a way to free an innocent Man and now afraid that he was tampering with powers beyond himself. Pilate wanted nothing of either of these circumstances. He simply wanted to be rid of this.

Let's not conclude that there is any spiritual insight with Pilate, however. He remained arrogant. He remained annoyed just as much as he was superstitious. And his presumption that this man or god or whatever he might be depended on him for his life proves he still had no idea who Jesus really was. He sought to release Jesus in a way to please the people, not for justice's sake. He sought Rome's compromise, and he sought some middle ground between truth and lie. But as all post-moderns and relativists eventually discover, there is no middle ground between right and wrong, between true and false, between salvation and condemnation, between the kingdom of God and the kingdom of man. The words of Jesus remain true, "Whoever denies me before men, him will I deny before the Father."

Johann Peter Lange, quoting Gossner, wrote, "Duty and fidelity towards God in one's conscience cannot be divided, else infidelity is already

---

5. Gorman, *The Last Hours of Jesus*, 187.

an accomplished fact."[6] That lesson can be learned from Pilate. Fidelity and infidelity are never served together. Once one has determined that he or she does not have to be faithful, infidelity has already occurred. It's just a matter of degrees and of who is hurt besides the one who is already serving two masters.

Jesus replied to him. He spoke to this judge who was so graciously offering to use his power to save the incarnate Lord. "You would have no authority over me at all unless it had been given you from above. Therefore he who delivered me over to you has the greater sin."

Saint Augustine noticed that Jesus said the one who delivered him had the greater sin, thus not exempting Pilate from guilt as well. Verse 12 teaches us that from that point Pilate applied himself to Jesus' release. I agree with Augustine that Pilate heard clearly that the guilt for an innocent man's death would be on him. Whether it is the greater or lesser sin, it is his sin nonetheless.

But the Jews pushed back just as hard as Pilate sought to have him released. They pushed back, and they introduced a threat now against Pilate himself. They announced that if Pilate allowed Jesus to go free, he was no friend of Rome. In fact, he would be an enemy of Rome. They now were bringing charges against Pilate that he himself could be brought up as one who was a seditionist. How ironic when Barabbas was a zealot, an enemy of Rome, the zealots would begin the uprising that resulted in the destruction of Jerusalem in 70 AD, and yet Pilate released Barabbas, but if he released Jesus, the Jews would accuse him of being an enemy of Caesar.

Pilate knew the emperor Tiberias quite well. A charge such as this would bring a severe response from Tiberias. Still, Pilate made another attempt to distract and dissuade the Jews, now leaning more into psychological play than he had actual legal parlance. But this last move of his in this terrible series of strategy and rhetoric and counter-strategy and rhetoric destroyed any further opportunity for the release of Jesus.

After their attempt to intimidate Pilate by mentioning his king, Pilate presented Jesus to them as theirs. His move, an insult to them, made the Jews cry louder for his crucifixion, and Pilate, losing his self-composure, destroyed any hope for Jesus' release, and fanned the flames of the agitated Jewish mob. With bitter sarcasm, he yelled out to them, "Shall I

---

6. Lange, *A Commentary on the Holy Scriptures*, 576.

crucify your king?" The chief priests had hoped for an opening just like this. Without hesitation, they claimed loyalty to Rome, and that they had no king but Caesar.

Now the tables were turned, and it was the Jewish Sanhedrin who were the defenders of the empire of this world, while Pilate was the last one standing between them and the Messiah. Perhaps it was with these words more than any other that Israel's rejection of their Messiah was most clear. "Our king is Caesar. Our kingdom is Rome." The trial is virtually concluded at this point. With no way out, Pilate stared down at the Jewish mob knowing that it was check and mate, and he had lost. There was no more doubt or hesitation. Pilate, ever the pragmatist, turned away from Jesus, abandoning him. Pilate put his period at the end of the sentence in our creed that reads, "He suffered under Pontius Pilate."

So, in about the sixth hour of the day, 12 noon, of Passover preparation, that is the day before Passover, in a place called Gabbatha, which means literally *high place*, in the palace Fortress of Antonia, Jesus was condemned.

Matthew tells us that Pilate took some water, and he washed his hands, symbolically testifying that this lynching of an innocent Man was their doing, and not his. How many have pretended that a few words, some symbolic act of reconciliation could wash their guilt away? How often have people relied on the passage of time to cause others to forget their egregious sin and have sought to saddle back up as if nothing had ever happened? How many times have people tried to wash sin away with the means of man and this world?

The teaching of all the Scriptures in both testaments is clear that sin and guilt are only washed away with the blood sacrifice of life. Sin is a crime against God, and his holiness is so perfect that any crime, the greater and the lesser, carries the penalty of death. In the Old Testament, a morning and an evening sacrifice reminded the people how serious sin was, but bulls and goats couldn't give satisfaction for man's sin—only the shedding of man's blood, and only that from a Man who himself was without stain or blemish or sin.

Robert Lowry, a popular Baptist minister in the late nineteenth century, put this scriptural truth to a song which has belonged to the Church ever since.

> What can wash away my sin?
> Nothing but the blood of Jesus;
> What can make me whole again?
> Nothing but the blood of Jesus.
>
> Nothing can for sin atone,
> Nothing but the blood of Jesus;
> Naught of good that I have done,
> Nothing but the blood of Jesus.

Pilate washed his hands, but his guilt remained. His captivity to sin remained. Had Jesus washed his feet, he himself would have been set free, but Pilate will have none of this ministry of Christ. He had turned Christ over to the wheels of Roman justice—the justice of this world that will always regard Christ with contempt. Will there ever be safe harbor in this world for Christ's Church? No, for this kingdom of God is not a kingdom of this world. It is alien, and it is foreign, and like antibodies in our own human bodies, any introduction of the kingdom of God in this world is fought hard as it would be an infection in the body, for it is antithetical to the principles and the purposes and the ambitions of everything that is in this world.

Pilate sought for justice. Perhaps there was some nobility in this man otherwise known as crass and callous, a hater of the Jews. And yet even his quest for some legal reconciliation failed in the end, and there was no way out. The kingdom of God remains antithetical to the world. It should not surprise us when the world says, "We want to hear nothing of the things of Christ." And yet our calling is clear. We bear testimony that it is not the washing away of our sin with water that makes us pure and acceptable to God. Nothing but the blood of Jesus.

Why must we enter into the drama of the passion? The Jews had the benefit of seeing a slaughter in the morning and a slaughter in the evening. We are indwelled with the Spirit of God, and we have the testimony of the Word of God before us, but if we close that testimony, then it would be the same as a Jew who refuses to ever go to Jerusalem for the Passover. We, in our human frailty, must be constantly reminded of the Cross of Christ, and of our own sin, and of his Passion. We must see it before us every day—every day—so that we can then call out and sing,

> Amazing Grace, how sweet the sound,
> That saved a wretch like me.
> We once were lost but now we're found,
> Was blind, but now we see.

12

Via Dolorosa

John 19:16–18

"So he . . ." that is, Pilate, ". . . delivered him . . ." that is, the Christ, ". . . over to them to be crucified. So they took Jesus, and he went out, bearing his own cross, to the place called The Place of a Skull, which in Aramaic is called Golgotha. There they crucified him, and with him two others, one on either side, and Jesus between them."

By verse 16 of Chapter 19, the trials of Jesus had concluded. Pilate had surrendered to the will of the Sanhedrin in turning Christ over for crucifixion. In this chapter, therefore, we will journey with our Lord to Golgotha.

A cross is a popular symbol today for both the Christian and the secularists. The cross, in fact, finds universal acceptance nearly any place you go unless it is being used specifically as a religious symbol. What place should the Cross occupy in the Christian life? What place does the Cross occupy in your own life? Entertainers often wear large diamond-studded crosses, hanging and prominently displayed on the outside of their clothing, even as they sing the most ungodly and vile lyrics. Crosses are used superstitiously to ward off evil spirits. People will hang them in places in their homes or use them as some way of divining and casting out evil spirits. They're used as a universally recognized symbol of the Christian Church as well, adorning the top of steeples or gracing the inside of sanctuaries.

It's a far cry in today's usage of the Cross from the words of Rome's most famous orator, Marcus Tullius, who said, "Even the mere word *cross* must remain far from not only the lips of the citizens of Rome, but also from their thoughts, their eyes, their ears."[1] Cicero once called crucifixion one of the most frightful punishments that human cruelty had every thought up. The historian Josephus called it "the most wretched of all ways of dying."

So how should we see the Cross today? This symbol which has been carried down through the ages since the crucifixion of Christ, is it a symbol of cursing, or is it a cherished symbol of our faith? Is it a proclamation of sorts, or is it something we should look at and turn our faces away from because of the curse that was placed there?

The practice of crucifixion itself seems to have originated with the Persians who refused to defile the earth with the body of a criminal, so they would place the criminal high up, and then allow the vultures and the birds to pick the bones until there was nothing left. Rome learned the practice from Carthage. It wasn't handed down from the Greeks. The Greeks seemed to have rejected the practice. So they learned this instead from Carthage, and they relied on it to maintain order and security in the outlying provinces of the empire. It was rarely discussed or even practiced in Rome proper, but certainly in the outlying provinces you found crucifixion to be an effective means of deterring a rebellion.

In turbulent Judea, crucifixion was common. Quintilius Varus crucified 2,000 Jews on one occasion. And during the siege of Jerusalem, 500 Jews were crucified every day during the siege in front of the city until it is said that there was no more wood to build crosses and that there was no more place to put them even if they had them. While crucifixion wasn't a punishment under Jewish law, Deuteronomy 21:23 does prescribe that one who is stoned to death should be hanged on a tree to show that he is particularly accursed by God. The Jews applied this in their idea of crucifixion.

In his work titled *The Suffering Savior*, Krummacher comments on Deuteronomy 21, noting this, "Such of them as were enlightened well knew that all this included in it a typical meaning and had a prophetic reference to One who should hang upon a tree, on whom heaven's wrath would be poured out, but in who's atoning sufferings the curse and condemnation of a sinful world would reach its termination."[2] Here he is saying simply, the Cross is the termination point in Christian theology of the

---

1. Marcus Tullius, quoted in Blinzler, *The Trial of Jesus*, 246.
2. Krummacher, *The Suffering Savior*, 161.

prophecies and of the types and the symbols relating to the wrath of God upon sinful man. Those who were stoned because they were an anathema to the Jewish community and because their sin would bring down the wrath of God upon the community, were stoned and then hanged on a tree so that it would be clear just how vile their sin was before God. And the Jews, taking that same symbolism and understanding, looked at crucifixion in the same way.

And so we find in crucifixion again the termination point of the understanding of God's wrath as all of Jewish history comes to this very point when they would hang One on a tree whom they considered to be One bringing down upon them the wrath of God, but whom we now understand and those who were enlightened understood was the Lamb of God who would take away God's wrath because he took away sin. The Jews of Jesus' time regarded the victim of crucifixion to be accursed over and above all other curses by God. We need to keep that in mind when we remember how urgently the Sanhedrin were pressing for crucifixion. Nothing else would do. It had to be crucifixion. They wanted the visible symbol of Christ hanging on a tree. They wanted that to fit into the theology of Jerusalem and of the Jews, that this One who claimed to be the Son of God was hung as One accursed by God.

In the new Christian Church, Paul would speak directly to this and put it in theological perspective. We have to wonder now in that first-century Church without the benefit of countless sermons on the Cross of Christ, without the benefit of countless written theologies and systematic theologies and studies that have been handed down age after age after age, without confessions of faith such as the Apostles' Creed and the Nicene Creed, what was the first-century Church to do with the idea that the One they called Messiah was hung on a tree, which in Deuteronomy seems to indicate that he was accursed by God?

Paul, in Galatians 3:13, said, "Christ redeemed us from the curse of the law by becoming a curse for us—for it is written, 'Cursed is everyone who is hanged on a tree'—" Paul doesn't dismiss Deuteronomy. He says, "Yes, indeed, there was a curse, and that curse was found on the Cross because Christ became a curse for us." So the symbolism remained intact, but through that One who became a curse also came forgiveness.

When Pilate delivered Jesus for crucifixion, it was getting very near midday. There was no appeal process. There was no second chance. There was no opportunity for overturning the verdict. And the journey from the Fortress Antonia to Calvary was some five to six hundred yards, not taking into account winding roads, hills and valleys.

Some conjecture that there would have been a second scourging as was very traditional before a crucifixion. One was sentenced to crucifixion, and then would be scourged prior to the crucifixion. Perhaps, if that's the case, then this would have been the worse of two scourgings. Perhaps the first, which was meant to convince the Jews that Jesus had paid enough of a penalty for their alleged crime, perhaps that would have been a more of a light scourging. This would have been the more severe. We don't know that there were actually two. It's not necessary that there would have been two. We do know there was at least one that was brutal.

No doubt the Sanhedrin pressed to have Jesus at Golgotha by noon because of the festival customs of the day, and if possible that the corpse would even be removed and placed in a tomb by sunset. Perhaps because of that rush, the Sanhedrin failed to notice the white tablet, whitened with a coating of gypsum that was either carried or hung around the neck of a condemned. All condemned carried such a sign which identified their crimes. We know Pilate listed Jesus' very specifically, that he was the King of the Jews. But there is no mention of that by the Sanhedrin until Jesus is finally at Golgotha.

John tells us Jesus kept the custom of carrying his own Cross. It may have been only the crossbeam Jesus was made to carry. That frequently was the case. The crossbeam would have weighed between 75 to 100 pounds. If He had to carry the entire Cross, it would have weighed at least 200 pounds, and probably more. The beam would have been placed on his shoulders. His arms may have been tied to hold it into place.

Two other men would join Jesus to walk to Golgotha on what is traditionally called the *Via Dolorosa*. Both are described in the same terms as Barabbas. They are called *robbers*, and that word that is used and translated as *robber* can also be translated as *insurrectionist*, which fits the scene more appropriately. Soldiers walked along. There would be a patrol in the front. There'd be a centurion who would follow, most likely on horseback. There would be armed patrols on each side, and then there would be a rear guard as well to keep down any opportunity for interference by the crowd.

From Antonia, Jesus walked through the gate and turned left. They would be taking the longer route to Golgotha because part of the Roman strategy was to expose this scene and this mockery to as many Jews as possible to discourage any future crime. They would parade their victims through the city, and they were taking him to the Ephraim gate, which was a thickly populated part of the city. At this time of the year, especially during the festivals, for Passover being the best attended festival, bazaars and vendors would be lining the streets. The upper floors above the vendors would be apartments and homes which now became box seats to the spectacle that was passing below.

I tried to imagine in my mind, *What do we have that could possibly compare to this?* Maybe you've been to Mardi Gras as people are partying in the streets. Or maybe you've been to some other festival which had vendors lining the streets, and the streets would be teeming and packed with people. And there, imagine in the midst of all of this celebration, as people from all around gather centrally into one city, you have someone dragging through a Cross going to be crucified. What a contrast!

The procession was nearly at an end when they reached Ephraim gate. They had only about a hundred yards beyond the gate that they would have to travel. There Jesus finally began to show signs of his mortality. We don't know if he stumbled or if he fell. In any case, the centurion recognized that he was struggling under the weight of the Cross. The remainder of the journey was uphill. The anguish of Gethsemane, the brutality, the beatings, the scourging, the lack of rest, of any fluid or food had finally taken their toll, and Jesus was faltering under the weight of the Cross.

The centurion was quick to act. He ordered Simon of Cyrene to carry the Cross of Christ. We don't know much about this mysterious figure, this Simon. He most likely migrated from Cyrene in northern Africa, between Egypt and Carthage. If so, he was probably influenced by the Cyrenic school of philosophy that taught rank hedonism, which is the pursuit of pleasure as life's highest good. Mark tells us that this man Simon was the father of Alexander and Rufus. It's interesting that they would include that detail except that we also know that Mark was writing for the Christian community in Rome, and it's likely that they were there and a part of the church. That would also complement Paul's request in Romans 16:13 that his greetings be extended to Rufus. It would make sense that Paul would extend a greeting to Rufus if Rufus was the son of the man who helped carry the Cross of Christ.

Thus Simon himself most likely became a Christian some time after he fulfilled literally and physically Jesus' admonition to take up his cross and follow him. Simon gives us our first glimpse of our own inward disposition as a cross bearer. The Cross of Christ must become ours through a process of self-accusation and a continual dying with him. This we call the *mortification of sin*.

We hear that term frequently. What does it mean? It means that we die daily to sin. We wage a war against the flesh. How do we wage that war? By self-accusation through introspection of the state of our own soul and our walk before the Lord, as we reflect on the admonition that we are to be holy as God is holy. We consider our own lives and we accuse ourselves of our own sin. Repenting of that, we then die to self, for we are united with him in a death like his. If we have been crucified with Christ, then we have been raised a new creation in Christ.

How terrible the weight of that Cross must have been when it was thrust across Simon's shoulders. How much heavier when Simon later felt the burden of his own sin. It's just as John Bunyan describes it in *The Pilgrim's Progress*. Shoulders hunched, the man plods through life, straining with every step to carry the great burden on his back. It has been a night and day companion. Not once has he known relief from its merciless weight.

The character John Bunyan writes of is named *Christian*, and he stumbles and struggles up a hill to where he sees a Cross, and as he arrives at the Cross, he sees there an open sepulcher, a tomb. And as he approaches the Cross and he surrenders himself to Christ, the straps on his pack which carries his sin begin to unravel, and it falls away, and the load of his sin falls into that open tomb never to be seen again. His sins are forgiven, and he is then dressed in splendid attire, the righteousness of Christ. Simon, in the picture, is that Christian slogging along under the weight of sin. When we have taken the Cross of Christ on ourselves, God will comfort and lift us up in union with the resurrected Lord.

From this point, Luke's account in his gospel points out that a considerable crowd was now following the condemned, all three of them. The onlookers added insult to injury by mocking the Lord. The crowd swelled to the point that three days later on Sunday, Cleopas remarked while traveling on the road to Emmaus where he walked with Jesus that even a stranger in Jerusalem couldn't be ignorant of the day of Christ's crucifixion.

Luke 23:27 does tell us that it wasn't his disciples who were in the crowd, however, but a group of women who mourned and lamented for him. We might have expected to hear of the disciples who were either there cowering or hiding or mourning, but there is no mention of the disciples. Perhaps John was there or Mark was there with Mary the mother of Jesus. They do appear at Golgotha. But what we do hear is of women who were there. We don't know who they were specifically, only that they were wailing and mourning for Jesus.

Jesus, now with the Cross on Simon's back, perhaps was able to stand more upright. Under the Cross, he would have been hunched over and not able to see so much of the crowd around him, but now perhaps he was able to stand more erect. He looks out and sees the women who are mourning and wailing and crying, and he says to them, "Do not weep for me, but weep for yourselves and for your children." Then referring to the destruction of Jerusalem, he says that they will see it as a curse on future generations. And he then said, "For if they do these things when the wood is green, what will happen when it is dry?"

In the first testament, a green tree was the symbol of a righteous and upright man. Here the green refers to Christ. If they will do this to the wood that is green, then what will they do to that dry wood, which is Jerusalem? The justice of God will reach out to Jesus. What will the wrath of God be against the people who have crucified the Lord? Jesus says to them, "No tears are shows of pity for me, but weep for your own condition, and weep for the future of your children."

Weep for ourselves as we watch? As Christ travels the road to Golgotha, we are told to weep for ourselves? Forty years later in one of the most horrible days of history, the city would be laid to waste in judgment, and the Jews who were there are either killed or sold into slavery. How often is the Passion of Christ presented, or told, or read? How often are we made to picture the story and the narrative of Christ, which is left incomplete, for we are left like the women who are mourning and wailing at the sad state of a beaten, bleeding Christ who stumbles under the weight of his own cross. How often are we left with that sense of despair and of shame or pity for the Lord? But the Lord would look and say, "Don't weep for me." He is not doing so simply as a statement of courage; the Lord saw clearly their own future, and he was saying to them, "If you knew your own future, you'd be weeping for yourselves, and you'd be weeping for your children, not for me."

The procession moved on through the gate. About a hundred yards outside the city walls, there was a place. It was elevated, and just to the right of the highway where all could see the gruesome executions as they travel back and forth, in and out of Jerusalem.

Scripture attaches great importance to his being led outside the gates. It's not simply because it was custom or because that just happened to be the place. Hebrews 13 ascribes great importance to the fact that Jesus was taken outside of the city gates. In Hebrews 13:11 and 12, we read, "For the bodies of those animals whose blood is brought into the holy places by the high priest as a sacrifice for sin are burned outside the camp. So Jesus also suffered outside the gate in order to sanctify the people through his own blood." If only the people of Jerusalem had eyes to see that this was the sin sacrifice whose blood was being spilt, and who would be taken outside the gate, just as they did in their practice of sacrifice for sin.

John omits any details about the actual crucifixion. Historical accounts give us plenty of detail. We won't dwell on them here except to say that we know Jesus was fastened to the Cross with spikes in his hands and his feet. The thieves traditionally would have been crucified in the same way. At times, criminals were tied to the cross, but on this occasion they were nailed to the crosses.

How strange the contrast with the manger. There, Jesus was born, surrounded by adoring shepherds, and angels in song, eventually to be visited by kings from the Orient and showered with gifts. Now he was surrounded by criminals and insults.

The two criminals hanging beside Jesus were just another expression of Pilate's disdain for the Jews. He put before them their King with two of the lowliest subjects of the kingdom. Through Pilate, the Word of God was being fulfilled however. In Isaiah 53:12, we learn that the One who would come, that is, Jesus who has come, was to be "numbered with the transgressors." And while the Jews had cast Jesus out, God, through Pilate, was associating Jesus again with his people. They had excommunicated Jesus through the trial, but now Pilate hung a sign above him that said, "He is the King of the Jews," and he placed beside him two Jewish insurrectionists.

So in the crucifixion, Pilate reintegrated Jesus again back into the Jewish community. This shows us the depth of Jesus' humiliation because even here on the Cross, he was surrounded only by words of scorn and the rabble of mankind. From the Cross, Jesus looked down on the sons of the first Adam, of those who were of the old creation, and his ears received their taunts and their complaints.

Even the thieves on their crosses joined in taunting the Lord. How like each of us as a sinner who searches out the blemish in another, just as those thieves hanging for their own crimes hurled taunts at the Lord. Even in our own sin, we can point to another, and would rather point to another, and reflect on their sin instead of our own. How much more we love to see the splinter in our neighbor's eye while ignoring the plank that is in our own.

We hear the words of the taunting thieves right down to this day. They said, "If you are the Messiah, if you're the Son of God, then why don't you save yourself, and why don't you save us?" Today, people say, "If God is real, then why doesn't he relieve my pain? Why doesn't he relieve my sickness? Why doesn't he remove this from me?" The scoffer, with a heart that is hardened in unbelief, is to be left to his fate.

But in the midst of the taunting, the Lord God pricked the heart and the conscience of one thief. Perhaps he grew silent as he began contemplating his own demise and the Man who was hanging beside him. As a probable zealot, he would have known of Jesus and his ministry. As he reflected on Jesus and the world that crucified him, he was moved to change his tone. Listen to his self-accusation. "This Man is innocent, but we are being punished for our own crime. We are receiving the due rewards for our deeds." He professed Jesus' innocence, and he claimed himself to be a sinner. Aren't these the very steps to salvation?

Jesus is the righteous One of God. I am a vile and unworthy sinner. And then a prayer. "Lord, remember me." This is the very moment we in the Christian Church pray for unbelievers—a moment of reflection, of introspection, and remembrance of Christ, and then a decision to say that this Man is innocent, but I am guilty, and I would be punished justly if I received what my deeds deserved, but Jesus is just and righteous. "Jesus, remember me when you come into your kingdom."

James Montgomery Boice quipped, "What did Jesus answer? Did Jesus say, 'It's too late for you now. You should have thought of that when you were joining the revolutionary band'? Did He say, 'I appreciate your confidence, but I don't know. If we get through this, I'll see what I can do for you'? Did ye say, 'We're both in the same boat, mister. We just have to grit our teeth and bear it'? We know he did not. Instead, he said in quiet confidence, 'I tell you the truth. Today, you will be with me in Paradise.'"[3]

What place do we conclude the Cross should occupy in the life of a contemporary Christian? Centuries ago, just off the coast of South China, the Portuguese built an enormous cathedral up on the top of a hill overlooking the Marco Harbor. On the front wall, they placed high up into the air a bronze cross, visible from many, many miles away. Only a few years later, a typhoon struck the south coast of China, and it swept the cathedral away, everything except the wall with the cross still high up in the air.

Centuries later, a ship would wreck outside of that harbor, just beyond the harbor, and it left very few survivors. John Bowring clung to wreckage without any idea where land was. And as the waves would come and swell and then recede, he would ride the wave up. And each time the wave would take him up high, he could see across the water the faint glimmer of a cross far in the distance. And he began to make his way to that cross. Later, Bowring would write these words:

> In the cross of Christ I glory, towering o'er the wrecks of time;
> All the light of sacred story gathers round its head sublime.
> When the woes of life o'ertake me, hopes deceive, and fears annoy,
> Never shall the cross forsake me. Lo! it glows with peace and joy."

Again, I'd like to quote Krummacher. "The experience of all who in faith take upon them the Cross of Christ agree in this that they are ever longer drawn into the death of him who hung upon the tree. They decrease. The more completely they suffer shipwreck as to everything they own, the more valuable the Cross becomes to them as the only plank of rescue from the surge. How fervently is it then again embraced. How lightly and loudly praised."[4]

What place does the Cross occupy in your life? Is it ornamental, an object of jewelry and home decoration? Is it an object of superstition where you want to make sure that you have a cross in your pocket, or you make sure that it's strategically placed to ward off evil spirits and demons? Or is the Cross the place where you are found daily confessing the Lord, both who he is and introspectively who you are, and then praying, "Lord God, remember me in your kingdom"?

---

3. Boice, *The Gospel of John*, 1498.
4. Krummacher, *The Suffering Savior*, 344.

13

King of the World

John 19:19-22

> Pilate also wrote an inscription and put it on the cross. It read, "Jesus of Nazareth, the King of the Jews." Many of the Jews read this inscription, for the place where Jesus was crucified was near the city, and it was written in Aramaic, in Latin, and in Greek. So the chief priests of the Jews said to Pilate, "Do not write, 'The King of the Jews,' but rather, 'This man said, I am King of the Jews.'" Pilate answered, "What I have written I have written."

From the reading of the four gospels, their accounts of the testimony of the life and the ministry of Jesus, we can conclude with some certainty that John alone actually witnessed the crucifixion. We don't know the whereabouts of the other apostles, but we can say with some certainty that John was there, and that John did in fact see the crucifixion scene with his own eyes.

John doesn't describe the actual Cross. It most certainly would have been a Cross on which there was a horizontal crossbeam placed in another vertical crossbeam that extended above the horizontal. It is possible that it could have been in the shape of a T which you sometimes see represented, but it was most likely that the Cross was just as we usually see it, a vertical beam and then a horizontal beam placed below the top of the vertical beam.

John gives us other details that are unique to himself which cause us to want to pay particular attention to how John describes the scene at the Cross. John recounts Simon being pressed into service to carry the Cross. He tells us of a tender moment when Jesus entrusts his very own Mary to John's care. He alone tells us of the two sayings from the Cross of "I thirst" and "It is finished," and of how a soldier thrust a spear into the side of Jesus and brought forth a mix of water and blood.

While all of the accounts include the posting of the charge against Jesus, only John tells us all the languages it was written in, Aramaic, Latin, and Greek. The detail is significant because it's a declaration of the nature of Christ's kingdom. It's a global kingdom. It's not just a local kingdom. Whenever you say *kingdom* now, there is a lot of energy that will be gathered around that word. There is a great deal of theological preoccupation in our day with the whole idea of kingdom.

I am often asked about my view of the kingdom. Am I pre-mil, or post-mil, or a-mil, or any mil at all? Sometimes I wonder if it would be nice just to have a mil. It's not just a matter of curiosity; it's a passionate area of discourse and speculation.

Recently I had an opportunity for just such speculation. I stood watching a television news account of some of the earthquakes we've been experiencing, and there was a minister of another denomination. He was watching the screen, and then he said almost out of hand, "Well I guess we'd better get ready." I looked at him, and I said, "Well, we're always supposed to ready, aren't we?" He said, "Oh yes, but I think it's fairly clear that the end is coming quickly."

Engaging in casual conversation, not seeking any confrontation, I asked him, "Well what do you mean? When do you think that's going to be?" almost in jest, expecting him to say, "Well no one knows for sure." And he did say that no one knows for sure except that he reads his Bible, and the Bible clearly says that when this begins to happen, that it's going to be pretty quick. I, of course, then countered and said, "Well, hasn't every generation thought that it was going to be their generation?" And certainly there have been worse times in human history than the times we now experience. And there have been times when nations have sought to build an entire global kingdom of their own. And alluding to, of course, the kingdoms that we see represented in the book of Revelation, a place where we don't necessarily find ourselves now.

But he was adamant, and he was sure, and he asserted again as he looked at me with a bit of an accusing tone and said, "I've read the Bible, and I know what it says about this." Now those of you who know me know that I don't take accusations of not reading the Bible very well. And so with the hairs on my neck beginning to stand up, a point in my life that I do try to resist, I told him, "Well, I bet you believe in the Rapture too, don't you." God only knows why I had to throw that on the table. Of course he believed in the Rapture. I knew that, or I wouldn't have said it. And not only the Rapture, but he is firmly pre-mil.

At the point I asked him, "So would you describe yourself as pre-mil, post-mil, or a-mil?" He looked at me with an inquisitive look, and it was clear he had never even heard the terms. That is where we find ourselves now. We find ourselves in an age where religious fiction has dictated theology without any consideration of the Scriptures themselves. This particular minister was absolutely uncompromisingly fixed upon a theology that he has never studied from the Word, or else he would at least be aware of some of the tensions in interpretation. He had no awareness of them at all. There seemed to be only one cut-and-dry answer.

I will say that at the conclusion of our conversation, it was collegial. We were discussing this with good tone and good fellowship together, and he did acknowledge there were some issues that perhaps he wasn't quite clear about, but nevertheless I'd better get ready. I assured him I would.

It seems there is too much talk of calendars now when it comes to the kingdom and not enough talk of Christ. Too much talk of dates and times and earthquakes and nations and not enough talk of Christ. Whatever your view of kingdom, you're going to need a King to have a kingdom. We need more discussion about Christ and less discussion about calendars.

Perhaps we should begin our thoughts about the kingdom by lifting our eyes to read the inscription that was on the very Cross of Christ which read, "Jesus of Nazareth, the King of the Jews," written in languages that all the world could understand. Pilate ordered that sign partly out of custom because the accusation had to be posted at the scene of the crucifixion. But let's not be misled or mistaken. It also was largely due to his desire to slap back at the Jewish leadership.

No sooner did the Sanhedrin read the sign on the cross than they asked that it be removed. They suggested that instead Jesus simply be described as One who presumed to be King of the Jews. Some argue for contradictions in the gospel writers at this point because the writers word the sign a little differently in Matthew, Mark, Luke and John. Matthew says, "This is Jesus, the King of the Jews." Mark says simply, "The King of the Jews," as does Luke, "This is the King of the Jews." John says, "Jesus of Nazareth, the King of the Jews." So which was it, and why the contradiction?

This is a riddle that is easily solved. The answer is simply, "It was in three languages." And those three languages were interpreted by the writers of Scripture. The writers of Scripture, in taking those words which were on the placard, all tell the same story. Whether they use the word "This is Jesus," or whether they simply say "Jesus, King of the Jews," it was related that Pilate placed a sign, and that sign read, "This is Jesus of Nazareth, King of the Jews." Whether it said all of those words or whether we have a paraphrase doesn't do any harm to the inspiration of the Scriptures.

Pilate was an instrument of God in that very moment. When they came and they asked him to change the sign, Pilate, being used as an instrument of God, refused them, and said, "What I have written stays written in three languages." With that sign, Pilate was legitimizing a charge against Jesus that even he himself didn't believe to be just. In that sense, the sign is a symbol of his sin. For Pilate to reveal the truth about Jesus is to reveal his own shame. Jesus told him, "I'm King. I am a King, and my kingdom is not of this world." Pilate knew what Jesus had said, and to place that there was tantamount to a confession of his own sin.

Pilate imagined he could do away with Jesus by making him King of some other man, by making him King of some other nation, by removing himself from any authority which Christ may have. Today you may hear the words, "It's true for you, but not for me," or "That's just your interpretation." The one who says such things is not discounting Jesus entirely, but rather is denying that Jesus has any authority over him. It's as if the person says, "That Man is King of your life, but he is not King of my life." That sign over Jesus was put there as a symbol of resentment, and it was read with resentment.

What Pilate meant when he wrote it was, "Jesus, King of the Jewish fanatics, crucified in the midst of Jews who should all thus be executed." What the Jews read when they looked at it was, "Jesus, the seditionist, a King of rebels." Pilate said, "What I have written." Pilate wrote it for the Jews, but God has written it for us.

Commentator William Hendriksen sums the whole thing up better than I ever could.

> It was God himself who in his wonderful providence had directed the hand of Pilate. This does not in any way make God responsible for Pilate's motives in writing the superscription, nor does it mean that God interpreted the title as the governor interpreted it, but the words as such were true. They were true in this sense that the

King of the Jews was crucified in order that he may be the King of a spiritual kingdom which recognizes no national or racial distinctions, a kingdom in which the Aramaic-speaking Jew, the Roman, and the Greek, yes the elect from every tribe, tongue, and people, and nation are the citizens.[1]

By the crucifixion and execution for being King of the Jews, Jesus became in actuality King of all the people of God. Pilate attempted to limit the lordship of Jesus by making him only King of the Jews when he is King of the entire world, yet by God's sovereign hand, the sign was posted in languages the entire world could read. And by that sign, his name was preached to all nations. The Great Commission perhaps began right there on Golgotha as the name of Christ who is King and Sovereign, a name by which every knee will bow, was proclaimed from that hilltop outside the city gates.

All three of those languages were spoken in Palestine. Aramaic was the common language of the country people. Latin was the language of the army. It was the official language of Rome. Greek was the common language of the whole empire. And so in these three languages, all people could be made to hear of Christ.

In those languages, we have the language of Israel which had given the world true religion, the religion which Jesus described when he told the woman at the well in Samaria that faith, hope, religion, and truth come from the Jews. Peter Lange sees the old world and the new world present in these languages. The old world is represented by the Aramaic, as they were still captivated and captured by law, and then in the Latin and Greek, the language in which the Scriptures went forward, we see a new world.

So this sign can be said to hang between two worlds, the ancient and the modern. It bridges and connects the prophecies of the first Testament to their fulfillment in the New. The sign stands over a path leading out of a nation and into the world. In Romans 11:15, Paul says as much when he says, "For if their rejection means the reconciliation of the world, what will their acceptance mean but life from the dead?" If the Jewish nation's rejection of Christ means the reconciliation of the world, then acceptance of Christ means life from the dead.

John told us in the beginning of his gospel that he intended to write about Jesus who was rejected by his own but received by the world. Isn't

---

1. Hendriksen, *Exposition of the Gospel According to John*, 428.

that what John the Baptist said when he testified, "Look! Behold the Lamb of God who comes to take away the sins of the world"? Isn't this what is recorded in John 3 when Jesus, talking with Nicodemus, said that the Lord would send his only begotten Son that whosoever should believe in him would have eternal life?

Jesus reached out to the Samaritans. He received the Greeks who were coming to seek him. And he praised the faith of a Roman Gentile soldier. In chapter 6 of the gospel of John, he is introduced as the Bread of life who is given for the life of the world. And in chapter 10, he speaks of a gathering of sheep who are not in the fold of Judaism, but a sheep from a flock that is outside of Judaism.

Throughout the gospel of John, the universal scope and sequence of the atonement and the consequence of the atonement is clear. But what of the Scriptures available to the Jews? Were they purposefully kept in the dark? Was there no way that their own Scriptures could have led them to understand and comprehend this would be their King? They had multiple indications from the first announcement of a Redeemer in Genesis 3:15 to the many messianic psalms and the prophecies in Isaiah in chapter 2 when he speaks of the sprout of the Lord, or chapter 7 when he speaks of the virgin birth, or in Isaiah 11 and 12 when he speaks of the twig of Jesse, or maybe in Daniel when he prophesies regarding the Son of Man, or in Zechariah 6 when he says this, "Thus says the LORD of hosts, 'Behold, the man whose name is the Branch: for he shall branch out from his place, and he shall build the temple of the LORD . . . and shall bear royal honor, and shall sit and rule on his throne . . .' And the crown shall be in the temple of the LORD."

Jesus was accused of saying, "Destroy this Temple, and I'll rebuild it in three days." And the sign over his head read, "Jesus, King of the Jews." From their own lips, the Jewish leadership announced the fulfillment of the prophecies concerning Christ. Their testimony against him was that he would be the fulfillment of the prophecies regarding the Temple of God. Their angst at him was that he claimed to be King of the Jews. Both prophecies, if they had only had eyes to see.

All the aspirations of a people who long to have God rescue them and dwell with them and to rule over them are gathered in the Person of Christ. When we pause to realize the universal scope of the atonement, we ought to be taken aback that our God is truly no respecter of persons or nationalities. He is no respecter; whether it be a man or a woman, rich or poor, slave or free, Jew or Gentile, white or black, Hindu, Buddhist, Muslim, the way is made open through Christ.

In Romans 2, Paul urges a circumcision of the heart over outward religious practices. The one who would pretend to be Christian is no more one who has circumcision of the heart than the Muslim who is estranged and far away from even the very name of Christ. Now there is another image Paul gives us in Colossians 2. "And you, who were dead in your trespasses and the uncircumcision of your flesh, God made alive together with him, having forgiven us all our trespasses, by canceling the record of debt that stood against us with its legal demands . . . ." And note, ". . . This he set aside, nailing it to the cross."

Our crime, our sin, the accusations against us were nailed to the Cross. Do you see the imagery Paul is giving us? A sign is placed on the Cross of One condemned to die by crucifixion. My sin is on a placard on his Cross. Paul is teaching about imputation, the imputation of my sin to Christ. The placard that would be over my head on my cross on my day of judgment was placed over his.

James Montgomery Boice wrote, "In him, our violation of God's just law was punished, and God can therefore reach out to justify the one who trusts him regardless of that person's nationality, intelligence, race, or any other factor."[2] In him, our violation of God's just law was punished.

If the placard on the Cross bridges the old world and the new, the Man to whom the placard refers bridges the old man and the new, the old Israel and the new, for any who will accept this as the truth, and listen carefully, that Jesus Christ will sit by God. His own Son was crucified as a substitution for the sinner to satisfy the perfect justice of God, and was raised again as the first fruits of the kingdom of God, and reigns now in his kingdom and in his people. He died for you. If that is what you believe, if that is your faith, then you are the one he died for.

Believing that Jesus died for you is faith. People often ask me, "What is faith?" They say, "Accept Christ by faith." If you know that Jesus Christ is the incarnation of God, if you know he lived and died on a Cross, and that your sin was placed on him, and that God now able to justify you, that is to declare you righteous, then you have received Christ by faith. If that is the testimony of your heart, for you don't call out to be saved on the basis of any of your own works or any of your own merit. You don't

2. Boice, *The Gospel of John*, 1505.

say that after death you simply cease to be. You acknowledge there is a judgment, you acknowledge there is a God, and you acknowledge there was a Cross by which God reconciled men to himself. If that is the truth that you know, then you have received Christ by faith.

If you have accepted Christ by faith as your Savior and King, then ask yourself if your life reflects his lordship and reign. If you say Jesus is Lord of your life, then what is he Lord of exactly? Your time? Your talents? Your money? Your career? Your family? Your passions? Your pursuits? Your ethical priorities? If you have claimed that you have received Christ by faith, then you are also claiming he is Lord and King and Sovereign of your life. And if that is your claim, then how does your life prove that your words are true?

Boice uses the placard itself to distinguish areas of life that we must submit to the lordship of Christ. The first language, Aramaic, was a language of the people in Jerusalem. It recognizes his kingship over religion because it was from the Jews that salvation came. He is the revelation of God, and as such, he alone can teach us the truth.

The second language, Greek, was a language used for science and culture and philosophy. If he is Lord of all of these, then he is Lord of culture, personal as well as corporate culture. The third is Latin, the language of law and government. Jesus has interpreted God's law and will return to judge those not abiding in him by that very same law. His law must govern our ethic and our life.

All the way to Golgotha, the Cross which our Savior dragged proved the character of those who passed. Most who saw him come by scorned at him, and they mocked him. They mocked at Jesus as he carried the cross along. Only a few wept and wailed. The placard over his head drew an even greater contemptuous response from the Jews, and it was a contemptuous Pilate who put it there.

When I say to you that your King is Christ, and you must return to him a life not your own but his, what is your response? What does the Cross show about you as it passes by? Does it show you to be a sinner, a sinner whose crimes have been nailed to the Cross? One way or another, you must deal with the Cross, and read the placard, and determine whether Jesus Christ is your King or not. May God grant each of us a proper reflection on our standing with Jesus of Nazareth, who is the King of the Jews.

14

Prophetic Fulfillment at Golgotha

John 19:23–24

> When the soldiers had crucified Jesus, they took his garments and divided them into four parts, one part for each soldier; they also took his tunic. But the tunic was seamless, woven in one piece from top to bottom, so they said to one another, "Let us not tear it, but cast lots for it to see whose it shall be." This was to fulfill the Scripture which says, "They divided my garments among them, and for my clothing they cast lots." So the soldiers did these things.

It is so tempting to distract ourselves, to avoid some of the issues on the hill where the Cross of Christ was set. It's a grim scene. There is no way that we can dress it up, and to do so would be to do an injustice to the Scriptures themselves.

We have reached a time of mourning in the gospel. Our Savior was crucified, and he was breathing nearly his last. The words which he spoke were nearly his last. It would be easy to gloss over these verses, to avoid the details of the Savior on the Cross, for in that we see our own shame.

When did you last hear a sermon or even a teaching of any substance on the passage where Christ's garments are stripped from his body, heaped into a pile, and distributed among the soldiers. I cannot recall hearing any in-depth treatment on this passage.

There is a general awareness of the dividing of the clothes of Christ as it is recorded in each of the gospels. All four writers record it for us thereby testifying that it is of significance. Yet, while there is a general awareness in the Church and among Christians of this event on Golgotha's hill, the passage as a whole seems to receive fairly slight attention. In contrast, I've heard numerous meditations, and there are even songs about the swaddling clothes of the nativity, but nothing on this tunic of Calvary. Are we uncomfortable with the indignity that is heaped upon Jesus as he is stripped and naked on the Cross, or do we simply have no theological framework?

Is this garment seamless? Some see here unity of the Church. Others see it as a testimony to Christ's High Priesthood because the priests themselves would have worn a very light garment. So in removing this from him at the Cross, theologians see a testimony that Christ is our High Priest. We can agree that there is certainly a unity to the Church, and we can also agree that the Scriptures strongly affirm the High Priesthood of Jesus.

One assumption that is often erroneously taught is that this tunic would have been of great value, and therefore, this proves Jesus was a Man of means, even of wealth. From this springs, whether we can believe it or not, an entire theology that is commonly referred to as the health-and-wealth gospel, showing that Jesus wore the equivalent of designer clothes in his day. That not only shows a complete misunderstanding of the balance of the Scriptures, but it also shows there is no comprehension of the culture of the Far East.

Our clothes are mass-produced. We get our clothes with a designer label so that we can say it came from this place or that as a testimony to how much we paid for it. It's a status symbol. But a tunic that was handmade from a loom in the Eastern culture at the turn of our century wouldn't have been an uncommon garment. So it would not bear testimony of designer clothing as some like to pretend that it does in our present day. Such a using of Christ to craft a theology of our own liking is an abomination.

I'm going to suggest to you that there is more here than just a record of our Savior's humiliation which is extremely important. This is a pictorial moment that we need to dwell on. It's a pictorial moment of prophetic fulfillment in the progress of redemptive history. We have here a picture of the doctrine of justification by faith in the stripping away of the Lord's clothing.

Most of us are familiar with the hymn story of Horatio Spafford who wrote the great hymn *It Is Well with My Soul*. After losing his children in the waters of the Atlantic Ocean, Spafford traveled that same route to meet his surviving wife in England. As he journeyed, the captain alerted him when they passed over the spot where his children lay on the ocean floor. No longer, in his mind, were they just out there somewhere, but they were right there just beneath him in the water.

When we study the doctrine of justification by faith alone, oftentimes we know in our heart of hearts it is true, and we are convinced by the testimony of Scripture that it is true and that it is real, just as Spafford knew before he boarded the ship that his daughters were out there somewhere underneath the waves and the water. But in this passage of Scripture, I believe we can say that we are passing over the very spot where an exchange took place. This exchange results in our being counted as righteous even as our Lord's suffering testifies and intensifies to its most extreme measure.

If we'd been present at Calvary on that day, and we had been observing as one not fully understanding all that was occurring on the Cross there in the center between the other two criminals, we would say that everything was proceeding quite normally. Nothing spectacular was happening as far as these things go on a day when people are being crucified. After the last duty of hoisting Jesus up onto the Cross, the guards were given a right to divide up the clothing of the crucified.

This was actually a Roman law that was called *De bonis damnatorum*, where they were able to take the clothes from the crucified, which clothes would be essentially bequeathed to the executioners as a sort of a last will and testament of those who were on the cross—a testimony that once the cross was erected, the victims were considered as already dead. Imagine the psychological and the emotional pain and anguish of those who were gasping for breaths of air while they watched their clothing being distributed as if they had already died.

The centurion, or the captain of the guard, would naturally or logically have the first choice of the condemned's clothes, but interestingly enough, as we learn from other passages, the centurion on this occasion had become preoccupied with One who was hanging on the Cross. Eventually he himself would arrive at a conclusion that surely this was the Son of God. The guards themselves, however, were simply fulfilling a prophecy in Psalm 22. And they fit the description well. They were hardly more than wild beasts.

It's easy for us to conclude that the 22nd Psalm is a vision of the crucifixion scene because Jesus quoted from the first verse saying, "My God, My God, why hast thou forsaken me?"

> "My God, my God, why have you forsaken me? Why are you so far from saving me, from the words of my groaning? O my God, I cry by day, but you do not answer, and by night, but I find no rest. Yet you are holy, enthroned on the praises of Israel. In you our fathers trusted; they trusted, and you delivered them. To you they cried and were rescued; in you they trusted and were not put to shame.
>
> "But I am a worm and not a man, scorned by mankind and despised by the people. All who see me mock me; they make mouths at me; they wag their heads; 'He trusts in the LORD; let him deliver him; let him rescue him, for he delights in him!'
>
> "Yet you are he who took me from the womb; you made me trust you at my mother's breasts. On you was I cast from my birth, and from my mother's womb you have been my God. Be not far from me, for trouble is near, and there is none to help.
>
> "Many bulls encompass me; strong bulls of Bashan surround me; they open wide their mouths at me, like a ravening and roaring lion. I am poured out like water, and all my bones are out of joint; my heart is like wax; it is melted within my breast; my strength is dried up like a potsherd, and my tongue sticks to my jaws; you lay me in the dust of death.
>
> "For dogs encompass me; a company of evildoers encircles me; they have pierced my hands and feet—I can count all my bones—they stare and gloat over me; they divide my garments among them, and for my clothing they cast lots."

Was Psalm 22 written a thousand years before the crucifixion? It sounds like an eyewitness account. But here we have it written from the pen of David a thousand years before the event in a time where David wouldn't have even known what the word *Rome* meant. David was speaking of somewhat of his own anxieties, of his own travails, and yet we have an account so descriptive that when we say in our creeds, "He descended into hell," can we not hear in the words, "But I am a worm and not a man, scorned by mankind, I cry out, and there is no help. I could count the bones in my body," the anguish of Christ recorded so clearly in Psalm 22?

It's easy to conclude that the 22nd Psalm is in fact a vision of the crucifixion scene because Jesus has already quoted from it and because the actions of the soldiers are so specific in literal fulfillment of the prophecy given by David there. Even in the smallest detail, this thousand-year-old prophecy of Christ is proven to be true. And when I say the smallest detail, it goes beyond what a cursory reading would actually demonstrate, for in Hebrew poetry, when you have two lines that are related—one here saying that they are dividing my clothes, and then the next one that they cast lots for my clothing—it's natural for that second line to elaborate or expand upon the first.

But here we have something quite unique because the first line, "They are dividing my clothes," is plural, as in many articles of clothing. And then it says, "And they cast lots for my clothing," which is singular. And in the account given of the scene at Golgotha, there is clothing that is heaped up, and it is being shared among the soldiers. That would have been everything from sandals, or a belt, or an over garment, anything that he might have had on, until finally they come to what would have been his undergarment, the tunic, which was seamless. That being an extra piece, rather than dividing it into four parts and all having nothing, they decide to cast lots for it so that it is given whole to one, and at least they have something of value.

The Roman guards, ignorant of Psalm 22, in the natural course of their day's work were instruments used of God to fulfill in the most literal sense a one thousand-year-old prophecy written by David. In the guards' view, it was as much chance as is the casting of lots, but we know that even in the casting of lots Proverbs 16:33 teaches, "The lot is cast into the lap, but its every decision is from the LORD."

I'm humored at times by folks who, in their zeal to preserve man's own sovereignty over God's, will sometimes present absurd arguments by saying things such as, "Well, is God really worried about what shirt that I wore today? Did God tell me what kind of shirt I needed to wear? Or how about how fast I drove to work? Was God in charge of how fast I was driving to work? I got a cold yesterday. Was God in charge of those types of things too?"

If you were a Roman guard, and you knew nothing of this Jewish religion and this One they called Messiah, and you were doing like you did at all other times, and you said, "It's time now for us to separate these clothes," and you started taking the clothes, and then you started to cast lots for the tunic, what would you have thought if had told you that it was prophesied one thousand years ago that on this day you would do exactly these things? Would you have thought to yourself that God was involved even in the smallest details of life?

Jesus taught us that God clothes the flowers of the field, that he takes note of every sparrow that is in the air. As one who is created in his own image, that is you and me, how much more will he take note and apply his providential care to us? Even rude and ignorant executioners are used of God to confirm his own sovereign hand.

John pushes that point when he says, "These things the soldiers did in order that the Scriptures would be fulfilled." Did they do this of their own free will? I doubt there was anything they could have taken more pleasure in at that moment than to strip these prisoners of their clothes, and to divide them up, and to cast lots for them. Of course, it's all they wanted to do. It was all that they had their minds on.

Did they do this because God sovereignly compelled them to? He committed them to perform that very act a thousand years before they were born. While Pilate declared Jesus to be a King, the soldiers demonstrated that he was the true David.

David was a son of Jesse, and Jesus was the true rod out of the stock of Jesse. David became king from humble beginnings; Jesus was born in a manger in Bethlehem. David was a shepherd who became king; Jesus is the good Shepherd who is King. Both would see their kingdoms expand by degrees from smaller to larger. David was a man after God's own heart; Jesus all the more so. David served as a prophet as well as king; Jesus is Prophet, Priest, and King. David was anointed around the age of 30, and Jesus entered his ministry at about the same time as he went into the waters to be baptized by John the Baptist and anointed with the Holy Spirit.

That is why so many of David's Psalms, such as Psalm 22, seem to speak more of Christ than David himself. That is why the Psalms, particularly those Psalms of David, are so applicable to our understanding of Christ.

Our first essential understanding then of the verses which we've read is that it shows us a proof of God's sovereign hand in the provision of our Redeemer who was crucified on Golgotha through prophetic fulfillment. Perhaps, however, that isn't the most important lesson of these two verses.

The second lesson concerns the actual shame and the suffering of our Lord. The purpose of this shame and suffering is not to induce sympathy on our part but rather so that we might come to understand the depths and the destructive nature of sin and the intensity of God's wrath against it.

When Jesus entered Jerusalem as a King, he had requisitioned a colt. A King has a right. Jesus said, "Get for me this colt," and the colt was provided. The King required the use of a colt to ride into Jerusalem that he might also have a room. So the King said, "I need a room," so that he might go in as our High Priest to prepare that meal of the new covenant.

The King was given the colt. The King requisitioned a room. When he rode into town, people hailed him as their King, and they threw their coats down as a carpet before them. They themselves took off their own garments and threw them down before Christ that he might use them as a carpet because he was King. Once he was hailed, but now his own clothes were being thrown into a heap along with those of two other criminals. Now he was mocked.

Klaas Schilder commented, "So thoughtlessly does the world throw Jesus' property about that a centurion doesn't even think it worth his trouble to ask whether there is anything in the heap worthy of his attention. And the soldiers, grinning because of the meager loot,"[1] agree at least to give some consideration to one useful article on the pile. This is the humiliation. This is the humiliating end of a Man who began life with the gifts of gold, and frankincense, and myrrh.

Now all the worldly possessions he has to bequeath are counted as nothing but rags, something not to be purchased, but to thrown in a pile to win in a contest of chance. So Jesus hangs between two thieves with nothing but perhaps—if historical records of crucifixions are to be believed—a small cloth that would cover him. Because of the modesty of the Jewish culture, the Romans sometimes accommodated such things.

There as he hung on the Cross with his clothing stripped away, watching the soldiers divide his garments among themselves, already counting him as dead, and Lord spoke the first words from the Cross, "Father, forgive them, for they know not what they do." There is nothing more that can be done to humiliate him. Jesus has continued his descent to hell. This nakedness and this shame is part and parcel with the punishment of God.

When sin first entered into the life of man, he sensed his nakedness, and he was ashamed. When God cast man out of paradise into a world that was now hostile against man, he gave him clothing, clothing as a protection, clothing as a buffer between man and a harsh world. And so now as the second Adam is about to suffer the final indignation owed to man, even that will be taken away, and the shame of nakedness once

---

1. Schilder, *Christ Crucified*, 179.

again is before God. As Hebrews 4:13 teaches, "No creature is hidden ... but all are naked and exposed to the eyes of him to whom we must give account."

The loss of covering is described in other parts of Scripture in the sense of judgment as well, as in Hosea 2:9. Here God describes his judgment and his indignation against the nations that have come against him, and he says, "Therefore I will take back my grain in its time, and my wine in its season, and I will take away my wool and my flax, which were to cover her nakedness." In this final indignation, we can hear the suffering of our Lord as he cries out, "My God, my God, why have you forsaken me?"

Hebrews 12:2 tells us Christ's disposition towards the Cross. "For the joy that was set before him endured the cross, despising the shame." Despising the shame. Do you now see the abandonment of Christ, the aloneness of Christ? Do you now see the suffering of Christ? It's not only in the physical agony that he was being made to feel, but because of the sin that settled upon Him, this righteous One of God had his clothing stripped away that in his nakedness he would represent man in his sin before God—man in his sin before God.

Here is the third and final lesson. Read 2 Corinthians 5:1 through 5.

> "For we know that if the tent that is our earthly home is destroyed, we have a building from God, a house not made with hands, eternal in the heavens. For in this tent we groan, longing to put on our heavenly dwelling, if indeed by putting it on we may not be found naked. For while we are still in this tent, we groan, being burdened—not that we would be unclothed, but that we would be further clothed, so that what is mortal may be swallowed up by life. He who has prepared us for this very thing is God."

Can you see now the picture of our justification and the nakedness of our Savior on the Cross? The second Adam was stripped of his clothes and hung naked under the judgment and wrath of God while we—we are clothed with his own perfect, seamless righteousness.

In Galatians 3:27, "For as many of you as were baptized into Christ have put on Christ." Christ put on the flesh of sinful man. We who are in Christ have put on Christ and his perfect righteousness. He put on our humanity, and he suffered humanity's shame in order that we might put him on and rejoice in his glory. This is what we see in this scene at

Prophetic Fulfillment at Golgotha 131

Golgotha. This is the picture of our justification by faith. A great exchange. An exchange of our shame for his glory.

This is his message to the Church. In Revelation 3:17 and 18, "For you say, I am rich, I have prospered, and I need nothing, not realizing that you are wretched, pitiable, poor, blind, and naked." Here he is speaking to the Church, and he is saying, "You who are wearing designer clothes as it were, you who do seem to have everything in life put together and all of your needs met, you say, 'I have no need.' But in the eyes of God, you are poor, and wretched, and naked still in your sin before me."

"I counsel you . . ." Revelation says, ". . . to buy from me gold refined by fire, so that you may be rich, and white garments so that you may clothe yourself and the shame of your nakedness may not be seen." Why has the Lord done this for us? The beauty of Psalm 22 helps us again. In verse 24, "For he has not despised or abhorred the affliction of the afflicted, and he has not hidden his face from him, but has heard, when he cried to him." We cried out to the Lord, and our prayers have been heard. Our Mediator has paid the price.

Where are you concerning justification by faith? Have you seen something in the Scriptures at Golgotha as our Savior has been stripped to be identified with our sin and our shame before God? Have you seen something there as you gazed at Christ in this humiliating condition knowing that it is your own? Have you sought, as Paul explains in Romans, chapter 3, to build around yourself a religion? Have you surrounded yourself with good church attendance, with versions of the Scripture? Do you hum the songs which you hear on the radio or that you have in your hymnbook? Do you speak good Christian speak and even have some apprehension of several different Christian doctrines, and yet . . . and yet—do not realize that you haven't come before the Lord and he sees you as naked?

Perhaps you wonder if it is necessary to actually repent in order to be saved? Can't you just say, "I believe," and not repent? The only answer I am able to give is that if you feel no compulsion to repent, then you actually have never come to understand your own shame and nakedness before God.

So what do you have to repent of? If you have nothing to repent of, then by all means, don't repent. But if in fact you are a sinner, and you are saved by grace, then surely there is something that you need to turn from in order to turn to Christ. When you hear the cry of a condemned man, do you know that it is the cry of a condemned race? "My God, my God, why hast thou forsaken me?"

It should break our heart to know that we will hear those words again—but not from our Savior. We will hear them from those who have not put on Christ. Are you covered by the righteousness of Christ? Come to Golgotha. Come to Golgotha and see the Cross. Confess the Lord is God, and you will also receive the same promise he gave at Golgotha that you will be with him in Paradise.

15

The Love of a Son

John 19:24b-27

> So the soldiers did these things, but standing by the cross of Jesus were his mother and his mother's sister, Mary the wife of Clopas, and Mary Magdalene. When Jesus saw his mother and the disciple whom he loved standing nearby, he said to his mother, "Woman, behold, your Son!" Then he said to the disciple, "Behold, your mother!" And from that hour the disciple took her to his own home."

Around the Cross a strange mix of people had gathered and were standing watch as the Savior died. The people had a multitude of emotions and reactions. The Roman guards were busy splitting up the bounty of clothing which they had received from the condemned. The Sanhedrin stared at the slouching form of Jesus, relishing their victory in his agony as his life energy continued to ebb from his bleeding body.

A group of women standing afar off would be still heard wailing in lamentation. And there standing at his feet were a small party of people, most notably two which were keeping a silent watch. As long as there was life in Jesus, they would not leave his side. They stood by him, the mother of Christ, other members of his family, and the disciple whom he loved, John. They give life to the words from the Song of Songs, "Many waters cannot quench love, neither can floods drown it."

Mary, the mother of Jesus, and John, the disciple Jesus loved, were witnessing the nightmare of their lives, but they would not turn away. They would remain by the Lord's side. Friedrich Krummacher wrote, "Among the beloved women beneath the Cross, there is one who especially demands our sympathy. It is the blessed one who bore the Man who bleeds on the Cross, the deeply stricken Mary."[1]

Though it was grievous for Eve to stand at the grave of her favorite son Abel, and still more so for the patriarch Jacob to behold the bloody garment of his son Joseph, yet what was their grief compared with that of the mother of our Lord at the foot of the Cross? It was promised to Mary early on that she would feel the stab of the sword in her heart because of the life of Christ. We have no record of her cries of agony however. We hear no record of her pleas for his pardon. In fact, John makes it clear that she is standing by. Standing. She is not wailing. She is not fallen or fainting away. Like a noble sentry, she stands by the dying form of her Son.

Jesus himself, occupied with his own physical and spiritual anguish, weakened beyond our imagination, still opens his eyes to see the two standing there gazing at him with cheeks wet with tears, with bewilderment most certainly in their eyes. His heart was full of sympathy still for those he saw. What a love is this that enabled Christ to express sympathy for others in the midst of his own suffering.

His words were few, but they were direct and communicated a tender concern for Mary. Jesus, proving that he loved them to the very end, gave her the most loved disciple to care for her, and to John, he gave the honor of taking Mary under his care as his own mother. We're told in the Scriptures that he took her home that very day. In doing this, Jesus did more than just keep his responsibilities as a Son. Jesus established a new fellowship.

Remember his words from Matthew 12:46 and following? Jesus was teaching, and after the initial enthusiasm began to wear off from his teaching, word made it back to the family, and the family, led by Mary his mother, came to Jesus. While he was teaching, they sent word in for Jesus, and said, "You tell him that his family is here," fully expecting that Jesus would respond to his mother's call and would leave.

But Jesus did not go out. Were they there to lend him support? Were they there to encourage him? Were they there to warn him? Where they there to talk him into ceasing this particular stratagem of his of teaching and speaking the way he was, and to return home and perhaps regroup or to gather a base of support? We're not sure what message they intended to convey, but Jesus says this. "And stretching out his hand toward his

---

1. Krummacher, *The Suffering Savior*, 401.

disciples, he said, 'Here are my mother and my brothers! For whoever does the will of my Father in heaven is my brother and sister and mother.'" Jesus began teaching at that point a new kind of fellowship, a new kind of relationship—one that was not based upon flesh, but one that was based upon the Spirit.

Now we need to ask a critical question. Why only mention Mary when there were other family members present? Mary, the wife of Clopas and Mary's sister-in-law, married to the man who was Joseph's brother, she was present. That made her the mother of John, the one who was the cousin of Jesus Christ. Salome, Mary's sister, Jesus' aunt is present, and of course Mary Magdalene, a sister by way of the Spirit.

Of all those present, Jesus chose only his mother to address, except for John, as his address to Mary was related to him. Note that this is the last word of Jesus from the Cross that is directed at man. He has already said, "Forgive them, for they know not what they do." This is in reference to his enemies, those who are afar off who are estranged from Jesus.

His second words from the Cross, "Today you will be with me in Paradise," addressed those who would become his friends. In fact, one even on that day said to Jesus, "Do not forget me," or rather, "Remember me when you come into your kingdom."

And now this one: "Woman, behold, your Son!" These sayings, these first three of seven sayings of Jesus from the Cross have reference to the second table of the law, that is, the table of the law that deals with loving our neighbor as ourselves. The remaining four expressions from the Cross all have reference to Jesus himself in relation to his confession that there is one true God. Love the Lord your God with all your heart, soul, and mind. There are no other gods before the one true God.

The reason Jesus addressed his mother was not to exalt her to the place of being the mother of the Church as some would suppose. According to Klaas Schilder, the reason for which Christ while dying directed his last statement given to men to his mother is that the law commanded him to do so. The law placed mother and father in the foreground in the second table of the commandments. Whoever does justice to father or mother has fulfilled the whole second table of the law and has in principle kept the first table also. What law am I speaking of? "Honor your father and your mother."

And so there is a very natural event where the eldest son ensures the continued welfare of his mother. But why John rather than the siblings?

Why turn to the apostle John, a cousin, instead of looking to his own siblings? Jesus' being the eldest, you would assume naturally that the next eldest would take concern for the mother rather than it being John. Here is where we actually see the heart of the matter.

Jesus is providing a substitute for himself. And by putting John in his own place, he is fulfilling the law in and for himself and in and for those he loves. In doing so, Jesus is concealing himself—concealing himself. He could have mentioned to her that in three days' time she would see him again. And for that matter, he could have taken this matter up after the resurrection if it was really a matter that was that crucial or important. Or he could have taken this matter up before he approached Golgotha. But he does it here in the moments of his death. He tells John, "Observe, or look here, at your mother."

Why do it here? Why do it with John? Why not give her some indication to not despair, because in three days she would see him again. Nothing of the sign of Jonah is explained. Nothing is mentioned at all except his own expiration and the substitution of John in her life for himself.

He is concealing himself, but he leaves them all with a sense of his going away with only the Scriptures as their support. It is concealed from John as well. Jesus had called him and his brother the sons of thunder, indicating that he would bring a great voice and a tumult to the world. John now looking at Mary wonders, *Is this going to be the extent of the work of the kingdom? Is this the great work of the sons of thunder in the kingdom of God, to care for a widow within the confines of the four walls of my home? Is this the great kingdom work I have been called to?*

Jesus conceals himself in order that seeing they may not see, and hearing they may not hear. The incarnate Christ is passing from the earth, and he chooses a substitute for himself in John. With Eve, Seth came as a substitute for Abel. But Jesus can't be replaced in the same way. He isn't *a* Son; he is *the* Son.

The key to unlocking this really lies in the book of Revelation 12. There is a woman in Revelation 12 that appears in heaven with the moon at her feet. She is in labor, and she gives birth to the One who will rule, and then who is taken up to God, and sits on the throne in heaven. Clearly, the writer is speaking here of Christ.

The dragon who is waiting there for her to give birth misses the opportunity in God's providence to destroy the Child who is born, the One who will rule. And so he tries instead to destroy the woman as she flees.

She goes into hiding so that she can get away from the dragon. Failing to destroy the woman, he then goes to make war on her many offspring.

Now who are we speaking of here? We know of the One who was Christ. Who is this woman, and who are the offspring? We know the dragon. That is Satan. We know the war. It's a spiritual warfare. The woman is Mary in giving birth to Christ, but more. We're talking about the Church. And who are the offspring? We are the offspring. Who is it that Satan has sought to destroy? The Church.

There is an analogy of faith as it were in Mary's giving birth to Christ, and in the birth of the Church, in the birth of saints. There is an analogy of faith there; Jesus makes a substitute for himself in John. Mary would not have authority over John. It would be John who has authority over Mary. John will be the substitute for Christ as Christ conceals himself until the resurrection, so on earth the apostleship is being established in the Church.

A continuity is being established in the Church, that they would care for the one who gave birth to Christ. Not because she is queen of heaven, not because she is a woman who is now to be exalted or to be prayed to, but because of the analogy of faith. We have here a beautiful picture as Jesus conceals himself as a Man in the flesh until he is resurrected being the first fruits of the Spirit. He conceals himself and provides a substitute.

This is the Church, and Christ is taking a representative head of the Church in John, concealing himself in this substitute. Mary is a member of his Church. She had to let go of Jesus and accept Christ. John is being ordained for his life work. Could he see it at the time? All he could see was the mother of Christ and that Christ was reaching out to the disciple whom he loved and said, "Look at your mother." And he felt the burden of that responsibility to cherish and to care for Mary who was now mourning the loss of her Son. But as the days continued to grow and the time continued to pass, it became clear that the apostleship of John was what Jesus was speaking of.

This wasn't of themselves, but of Christ concealed in them. Jesus relinquishes his mother, and his ties to her are no longer of the flesh but of the Spirit. Who is my mother? Who is my brother? Who is my sister? The one who does the will of My Father." Jesus was establishing a new fellowship, a new relationship that would be based upon him in his people, a relationship based upon the erection of the Church and the establishment of the Church which would function under his authority as proved by the apostles in the first days of ministry.

"Behold, your Son! . . . Behold, your mother!" Behold your son in Jesus Christ. Behold your mother, the Church. John Calvin called the Church the mother of all Christians and said that no one could find life outside of the Church. The ancient saints, the ones who spent their entire lives studying the Scripture, who would spend more time in a month studying the Scripture than many of us do in an entire lifetime, used language that now is cloaked in more mystery than even the Scriptures themselves to us. Were they trying to be cryptic? Were they trying to be mysterious? No. They were trying to reveal the teaching of Scripture. But it remains a mystery to us because we so skim the surface of the Scriptures that the whole concept of mother Church and life and Christ in the Church don't resonate as it should with us.

And so when we hear the story of Jesus' words to Mary, we only think of it in an entirely human realm. *Here was a moment,* we think to ourselves, *when Jesus looks down and sees his poor mother, and takes pity on her. He sees John, and he trusts John, and so he says, "John, will you please take care of my mother? And Mary, my mother, will you please commit yourself unto John as if he was your own son?"* And we never ask the question about the other siblings. We never wonder why John and why Jesus with everything else going on wouldn't have either taken care of it before or said, "Mother, don't mourn. In three days, you'll see me again." We don't ask these questions. They don't occur to us. But in asking them, we find an answer.

Then we flip to Revelation, and we read, and we're mystified, and we make up analogies and allegories from Revelation because we have no concept of what the rest of the teaching of Scripture is to be. And so we have Revelation standing alone as a wonderful story full of mystical creatures. But all of it is dependent upon and ties into the rest of Scripture.

The book of Revelation should be the very last book which we undertake to study. It can never be understood unless the rest of Scripture is understood before. If you don't understand the Church, then nothing else in Revelation will make any sense. It's talking about the Church—the Church that is preserved, the Church that is saved, the Church in which Christ resides, the Church which is victorious, the Church which is the kingdom of God, the Church to which Christ will return.

Jesus concealed himself not from his own people, but he backed away from his life in the flesh that in three days time he would emerge again the first fruits of the new kingdom. And the Church was established.

16

I Thirst

John 19:28–29

> After this, Jesus, knowing that all was now finished, said (to fulfill the Scripture), 'I thirst.' A jar full of sour wine stood there, so they put a sponge full of the sour wine on a hyssop branch and held it to his mouth.

It was about the ninth hour, or in our reckoning about three in the afternoon. From the companion gospels, we know that Jesus has already cried out, "My God, my God, why hast thou forsaken me?" And then a darkness had settled into the land. A darkness had settled into the bleeding form of Christ as well. Alone in his suffering, he uttered these simple words, "I thirst." In saying this, our Lord showed his suffering, and by our reading of Psalm 69, we know these words signal his resignation to wait, in fact, calling for death.

Psalm 69, verses 1 to 3 and verse 21 are literally fulfilled in these words here at the Cross. Not enough could be said regarding the prophetic fulfillment in every step of Christ's Passion. Not enough could be said, not enough sermons can be preached to grant to you a perfect assurance and understanding that all that was done had been ordered by God.

It was God-ordained that our Lord was there at Golgotha. It wasn't a tragic mishap, or a mistake, or a misunderstanding by the Jews that put him there. It was ordained by the Lord in literal fulfillment of prophecies, many prophecies throughout the Old Testament. And it also shows that all that has come to pass gives to us a striking display of Christ's perfect obedience because our Lord Jesus Christ was never caught by surprise in the events which he endured; he knew the Cross was his destiny from the very beginning.

He knew the Cross was his destiny when he divested himself of that glory which belonged to God and took on himself the form of human flesh. He knew the Cross was his destination and that the suffering of the Cross was his to endure. It was the cup which he said, "If there is any way, let it pass from me, and yet not my will but thine be done." He in his perfect obedience and omniscience had a full vision because of all of these prophecies. He knew the suffering he would endure. There we have a picture of that obedience which is perfect righteousness before the Lord.

Because Jesus knew his beginnings and end, he knew his cup of suffering was nearly emptied. But his suffering was not complete until the last dregs had been consumed. Just what was his suffering at this point? His thirst is certainly an indication to us that his suffering was real, and it was physical. Through sweat and extreme blood loss, Jesus would have been severely dehydrated at this point. His last drink most likely would have come at the Passover meal. Through the abuse that he had received throughout the trials, through the scourging and the great loss of blood, through the long walk carrying his Cross, through Golgotha and the sweat that would have occurred there, all of that would have served to dehydrate him in the extreme.

After arriving at Golgotha, he lost even more blood in the crucifixion itself as he was nailed to the Cross and hung there. He had been there for nearly six hours, his body almost immobile, the blood thickening in his veins, congealing almost. Here, very nearly to the end, his body hot with fever from the trauma, his tongue parched, sticking to his mouth, his lips cracking and bleeding.

Those who have experienced extreme thirst can have some empathy for what he was going through, though I would submit to you that since he was near death at this point, none of us here would have experienced thirst to this extreme. But any of us who have experienced extreme thirst without water being available remember it. We remember a time when we began to feel panicky because we did not have anything to drink, and there was within our body a screaming out for relief by means of water.

Some of said that in the time of their most extreme thirst—and many of these stories come from those who have had treks across desert lands—if they had all the gold in the world they would have traded it for one cup of water. They would have given all their possessions for just a few drops of the muddiest water from the filthiest pool. This tells us that even in these last moments, our Lord's incarnation was not spared any suffering. He took all of it.

He took all of the suffering, just as we would read in Psalm 22:14 and 15. Here it gives us a word picture of Christ's suffering. "I am poured out like water, and all my bones are out of joint; my heart is like wax; it is melted within my breast; my strength is dried up like a potsherd, and my tongue sticks to my jaws; you lay me in the dust of death."

Neither God nor angels thirst. Revelation 7:16 assures us that when we are raised in glory, we shall neither hunger nor thirst. But in our present condition, in our humanity, we suffer both hunger and thirst. And in his humanity, Jesus was not spared any of this. He suffered hunger, and he suffered thirst, affirming the words of Hebrews 2:17. "Therefore He had to be made like His brothers in every respect." And so here in the dying human form of Jesus Christ we have suffering in its extreme.

But it's not only his physical condition we need to consider. It's not only his physical condition as horrible and heartbreaking as it is because there is in the Scriptures another suffering that is explained. There is another in the Scriptures that complained of his thirst as well. He complained to Abraham and Lazarus—Lazarus, you remember, who rested in Abraham's bosom. A rich man who had a gulf that separated him from the blessings which the poor man, Lazarus, had in Abraham's bosom. A rich man who is in his life had never suffered thirst, but in the life after couldn't find a drop to give him relief.

Yes, the thirst of Christ is two-fold. He suffered physically, but He also suffered in his soul. We have then these three—a prophetic fulfillment that is given to us in these words, "I thirst." We have an indication and evidence of a physical torment that Jesus is made to undergo. But we also have here a testimony of the anguish that is in his soul.

Just before Jesus uttered these words, God had caused a darkness to settle on Israel, a darkness that is recorded in the other gospels. Matthew 27:45 reports that "From the sixth hour there was darkness over all the land until the ninth hour." Three hours of darkness that remind us of the three days of darkness in Egypt just before the firstborn were killed. Now three days until the firstborn was killed, in Golgotha turns into the three hours of darkness—the darkness that is associated with judgment when the sixth seal is broken as we read in Revelation, chapter 6, verses 12 and 13.

"When he opened the sixth seal, I looked, and behold, there was a great earthquake, and the sun became black as sackcloth, the full moon became like blood, 13and the stars of the sky fell to the earth as the fig tree sheds its winter fruit when shaken by a gale." Here we have a darkness that is associated with a judgment—a judgment considered in verse 17 of Revelation 6 to be the great day of their wrath. A darkness had settled on the land. It could be observed by all, but it was keenly felt by the Lord. Light was the first creation of God, the first creation as he brought order to chaos, to the nothing that existed as nonexistence. His light remained with man, and ultimately God himself promises and is described to be the light of man. But light is what is denied Christ here. God permits his Son to be swallowed up by that outer darkness that points ahead to the end of the world. In God's wrath even this first gift of creation, this first gift which God gave of light, is taken away, and Jesus is put outside of God's presence.

In Joel 2, verse 10, we read, "The sun and the moon are darkened, and the stars withdraw their shining . . . For the day of the LORD is great . . . who can endure it?" Again, the prophecy shows to us that great day of the terrible wrath of God when darkness overcomes the people. In Isaiah 13, he speaks of it as well in verses 9 and 10. "Behold, the day of the LORD comes, cruel, with wrath and fierce anger, to make the land a desolation and to destroy its sinners from it. For the stars of the heavens and their constellations will not give their light; the sun will be dark at its rising, and the moon will not shed its light."

As Klaas Schilder, who died in 1952, a theologian of the Reformed Church of the Netherlands, put it, "The day of the Lord has been in Christ's soul."[1] The day of the Lord has been in Christ's soul. It's not the length of the time of darkness, but its depth that our Lord was made to feel. As men die, it is said that their life flashes before their eyes. In the soul of Christ, all of human history was before him, from the forbidden fruit to Golgotha and beyond to this very day and until the last. My life and your life were flashed before his eyes. All the sin of mankind flashed before the eyes of our Lord. Every sin of every day was his only company in the darkness.

---

1. Schilder, *Christ on Trial*, 379.

Have you ever wondered what it meant to say that Jesus descended into hell? Well, here it is. It's been before us all along. Now do you hear him cry out, "Eli, Eli, lama sabachthani? My God, my God, why hast thou forsaken me? Why hast thou cast me out? Why hast thou cast me from your presence? Why am I made to dwell in the darkness?"

But the darkness is lifted and the suffering is done. Christ now only has to die. And he thirsts. The end is near.

He thirsts for the refreshment and relief that water will bring, and he thirsts for the end of his toiling. As the deer pants for the water, so his soul longs for communion with the heavenly Father. We might not know this if Psalm 69 wasn't so plainly spoken. "Save me, O God! For the waters have come up to my neck. I sink in deep mire, where there is no foothold; I have come into deep waters, and the flood sweeps over me. I am weary with my crying out; my throat is parched. My eyes grow dim with waiting for my God."

Our Lord was growing weak. He was growing faint. He had suffered the punishment for sin. He had been cast away from God. He had called out to the Lord. His body was wracked with pain and suffering and weakness. We know there was more than physical thirst involved because John tells us that Jesus knew the end had come and that He was acting to fulfill the Scriptures.

What Scripture was in the mind of Jesus? Psalm 69:21: "For my thirst they gave me sour wine to drink." This is the last prophecy. When he takes a little of the drink, he will die. This is the last act which Jesus will perform, save the act of death itself.

Don't imagine that this detail is unimportant. As Schilder points out, "He follows the direction pointed out in the Scriptures. It is a small indication hidden, often forgotten, lodged between so many other words, but in that tiny indication Christ's whole life is opened up for us, for precisely in the manner in which he died, he had ever lived."[2] Our Lord lived to obey and to do the will of the Father, and even as he emerged from that period of darkness, and even as he simply called for something to quench his parched mouth, he did so in obedience to the Father.

In his descent, his body suffered as well as his soul. The cost was extreme for the victory to be won. It was accomplished, and Jesus now knew that the end had arrived when he would surrender his mortal body

2 Ibid., 430.

up to death. The last part of sin's penalty having arrived, he had suffered the second death, the lake of fire burning with fire and sulfur in darkness. He now prepared to experience the first death.

Here now is our High Priest about to make the last sacrifice in carrying out his official duties as our Priest. In his final service before God, he desires refreshment and a moment's strength. Again, the words of Schilder as he follows this through: "He will not lose mastery of himself. He exerts his effort to command his last powers. Exhaustion is not to put him into death. . . . He calls his forces back into play, clears the eye, resembles Jonathan's last tasting of honey. Vinegar is good in order to fight to the very last."[3]

In other words, our Lord will not simply succumb to death by fainting of exhaustion. He calls out for drink to refresh, to bring his eye back clear again that he might in all fullness of whatever strength remains and with clarity of mind perform the office of High Priest in making this sacrifice before the Lord. How noble is our High Priest. How faithful to the end to deliver himself a fit sacrifice for the sins of man.

He refused the drink of wine that was offered to him before when he could have taken the cup with his own hand, and he could have drunk it because it would have dulled his senses, but he takes the drink now even if it is at the hand of another that he might gather himself for service to the Lord. The Scripture tells us that Jesus knew that all was finished before he asked for the drink. Here we see his resolution, his courage, his love, his love for the Father, and his love for us.

Having fought death, we would be tempted simply to succumb and grow faint, seeing that as mercy. "Lord, take my consciousness away. Let me die in my sleep." But not our Lord. Out of love for the Father and out of love for us, he undertakes to refresh himself for just a moment that he would present his own body the final sacrifice for sin.

Not a word of spite is uttered against those who have caused his suffering. "I thirst." He has prayed for his executioners, "Father, forgive them." He has opened his arms to the condemned. "Today you will be with me in Paradise." And now Abraham comes, not denying, but granting a drink in the person of a Roman soldier.

The work is done. Our Lord suffered and burned with thirst in order that we could drink living waters and never thirst again. We all have ex-

---

3. Ibid, 438.

perienced physical thirst from time to time. What if you were thirsty and did nothing about it? What if your body was calling out for drink, and you determined to ignore it? Or even worse, what if like a leper who feels nothing in their physical body you were not even aware that you were thirsting to death? How tragic would it be to die of thirst when water was available?

We still remember when we were thirsty and had nothing to drink if we've experienced that. So I wonder if we are putting our souls in jeopardy of experiencing a thirst that can never be quenched by ignoring the thirst of our soul and the quenching of the living waters of Christ. Are we ready for eternity, knowing that wrath which was intended for us has already been exhausted on Christ? Is that our understanding? Do we hunger and thirst for righteousness? If you hunger and thirst for righteousness, you will be filled. Christ is our righteousness.

And so our invitation is to come to the living waters, and you will never have a thirst of the soul. Come to Christ for his thirst was in your place. His suffering was in your place. His descent into darkness was in your place. The punishment which was meted out to him was the one that was for us. He suffered thirst, and he now offers you to drink from him as living waters that you would never thirst again.

17

The Sixth Word from the Cross

John 19:30

> When Jesus had received the sour wine, he said, "It is finished," and he bowed his head and gave up his spirit.

"Is is finished." The last words of our Savior before this had been, "My God, My God, why hast thou forsaken me?" and also, "I thirst." Now we go from words of lament and sorrow to words of joy—words of joy. If F. W. Krummacker is right, these are the greatest and most momentous words that have ever been spoken since the beginning of the world. Is that religious rhetoric, or is it true that these are the most important words spoken since the beginning of all creation?

James Montgomery Boice remarked that these words were "a triumphant declaration that the turning point in history had been reached and that the work that Jesus had been sent into the world to do had been done."[1] Before we explore how these words merit such lofty reviews by great biblical scholars, even to say that they are more important than any other words, let's turn our eyes of faith once more, albeit briefly, to the form of Christ who was still lingering there on the Cross.

Our journey thus far has been downward, downward, downward from the betrayal and the arrest to the trials, and from the trials down the Via Dolorosa to Golgotha. Golgotha, there crucified. Crucified after the scourging, the pain, and the agony, and the anguish, and the bleeding. The forgiving of his enemies. The promise of Paradise to those who repent. The promise of one who would watch after his own mother as Christ

---

1. Boice, *The Gospel of John*, 48.

began to hide himself and began to fade. The time of darkness where he hanged silent there on the Cross. "My God, My God, why hast thou forsaken me?" And then finally his thirst as he is made to drink vinegar.

But now we have a change of direction. With a great cry, Jesus says, "It is finished." The words you hear coming from our Savior are not the words of a defeated Man. They are not the words of a desperate Man. There is no despair, nor is there any fatalism in his tone.

Mark 15, verse 37 tells us that after Jesus had taken a drink from the sponge, he cried out with a loud cry—with a loud cry, a victorious cry. In the Greek, that cry is but one word, *tetelestai*. A loud cry is a sound of victory not defeat. The English translation really doesn't fully capture the essence of that one word *tetelestai*.

The Greeks considered it to be great oratory if you could compress great meaning and volumes of meaning and fact into a single word. They thought it was good oratory to be able to deliver a sea of matter in a drop of language.

In that word *tetelestai* is the gospel. In that word *tetelestai* is our assurance. In that word *tetelestai* is our joy and our consolation. It comes from a root verb *teleo* which means the completion or carrying out of a task. In the context of religious duty such as what Christ has been accomplishing, it means a person has completed and fulfilled all of their religious duties.

As Arthur W. Pink observed, "The Cross has two sides to it. It showed the profound depths of his . . ." that is Christ's, ". . . humiliation, but it also marked the goal of the incarnation, the completion of the work."[2] So, yes, we have dwelt, and rightly so, upon the humiliation and the suffering of Christ. That is one side of the Cross. But also at the Cross we find the culmination of his work, the whole reason for the incarnation, the whole reason and destiny of his entire life. And now he claims his work is complete. *"It is finished."*

Jesus has not been the victim of a crucifixion, at least not in the sense that he was victimized against his will because every step was according to the Father's plan of redemption set out long ago and prophetically spoken of through the ages. Jesus spoke often of his deliberate intention to fulfill all things by making atonement and becoming a propitiation for sin. And so Jesus speaking as both Prophet and Priest utters a single word

---

2. Pink, *The Seven Sayings of the Savior on the Cross*, 102.

that is the most important in human history, *tetelestai*, "It is complete," or "*It is finished.*"

That is why he utters it as a victorious cry rather than as a poor or weak and dying man. He calls out as the Lamb of God still possessing the heart of a lion. And as we read in the gospels, he added, "Into thy hand I commit my Spirit." Notice the difference in his prayer and that of Stephen the martyr who gazing into heaven prayed aptly that God would receive his spirit. "Lord, receive my spirit," Stephen prayed, but Jesus is uttering a committal for himself rather than a petition unto God. He is saying, "Unto thy hands I commit my spirit."

Johann Peter Lange, a man whose heart was enflamed with his love of Christ as he dwelt upon the Passion of Christ, gives an excellent summary.

> Finished was his holy life. With his life, his struggle. With his struggle, his work. With his work, the redemption. With the redemption, the foundation of the new world. With this triumphant cry, he confirmed the gospel to his disciples, the gospel which he announced to them and had bestowed on the world.
>
> In this one word, he once more comprised all that he had said to them in the High Priestly prayer. This word was his last to man. John kept it in his heart and delivered it to the Church as the great word of his farewell to humanity.[3]

Is all of this packaged in that one word *tetelestai*? Can we truly say that in this one word is a summary of all of our Christian faith, of all of the work of the Christ, of the very gospel itself? Yes, and by implication the cardinal doctrines of the gospel, mainly justification by faith alone. "It is finished," he said.

So the question that naturally follows is, so what was finished? If "*It is finished*," what is it that is finished? First we can say that his suffering was finished. And in that sense, in his suffering he is called a Man of sorrows. That is finished. In that sense we can hear in the word a tone of joy in that his suffering is complete.

He had hung on the Cross in the hellish darkness that swallowed him. In virtual silence he had hung there, except for the sad cry of, "My God, my God, why have you forsaken me?" as Satan bruised his heel. He had anticipated this his whole life. He had even read of it and learned of

---

3. Lange, *A Commentary on the Holy Scriptures*, 319.

it from his Father's Book, Psalm 88:15, "Afflicted and close to death from my youth up, I suffer your terrors; I am helpless."

At the wedding at Cana, he had said that his hour had not yet come. When he spoke with Nicodemus, he spoke there of his being lifted up. When James and John were discussing with him and debating with themselves who would be greatest in the kingdom of God, Jesus assured them there was a cup he had yet to drink and a baptism he had yet to undergo.

But now the silence is past, and he has something new to say. His suffering is at an end. His humiliation is nearly complete. The cup that had been set before him to drink is now dry, and he sets it down in its place, and he proclaims *tetelestai*, "It is finished."

A. W. Pink reflects on this, saying, "Now the suffering is ended. That from which his holy soul shrank is over. The Lord has bruised him, and man and the devil have done their worst. The cup has been drained. The awful storm of God's wrath has just spent itself. The wages of sin have been paid."[4]

But notice that Jesus doesn't say, "I am finished." As a Servant of God still serving, he is considering not himself but the work of God. He isn't drawing glory to himself by announcing his own faithfulness, his own fidelity to the purposes of God. He isn't drawing any attention to himself and for his success and his courage in enduring the trials set before him and drinking the cup which God had prepared for him.

His attention remains on the work the Father had given him to do. And even in this, Jesus consciously draws us back to the last verses of Psalm 22 to show us what he has accomplished. Psalm 22:31: "They shall come and proclaim his righteousness to a people yet unborn, that he has done it." Done what? We who are the ones spoken of in the Psalm, those who were yet unborn but now born, we are the ones that Psalm 22 is speaking of. And so now we ask, *What is it that he was done with?*

Some want to limit his work and his saying, "It is finished," to his proclaiming he had fulfilled all prophecy, that he fulfilled those prophecies that were given and spoken of him, of which there were many. But we know that there is yet a prophecy regarding his committal, in Psalm 31:5, which he has not yet uttered at the time he says *tetelestai*, "It is finished."

There is a prophecy concerning the piercing of his side in Zechariah 12:10 that remains to be completed. And the prophecy regarding the fact

---

4. Pink, *The Seven Sayings of the Savior on the Cross*, 102.

that there would be no unbroken bones as the soldiers come to break the knees of those who are still lingering on the Cross but discover our Lord has already passed. Isaiah 53:9 tells us prophetically that his would not be broken, and indeed, they were not.

But he is certainly done in the sense of prophetic fulfillment. The following table shows the Old Testament prophecy and the corresponding record of fulfillment in the New Testament.

The Redeemer will born of a woman's seed.
Prophesied: Genesis 3:15   Recorded: Galatians 4:4

The Messiah will have a virgin mother.
Prophesied: Isaiah 7:14   Recorded: Matthew 1:18

He will be s seed of Abraham.
Prophesied: Genesis 22:18   Recorded: Matthew 1:1

He will be of the line of David.
Prophesied: II Samuel 7:12, 13   Recorded: Romans 1:3

He would be named before his birth.
Prophesied: Isaiah 49:1   Recorded: Luke 1

The Redeemer would be born in Bethlehem.
Prophesied: Micah 5:2   Recorded: numerous references

He would bear the sorrow of others.
Prophesied: Jeremiah 31:15   Recorded: Matthew 2:16–18

He would be taken in flight to Egypt.
Prophesied: Hosea 11:1   Recorded: Matthew 2

He would have a forerunner.
Prophesied: Malachi 3:1   Identified in NT as John the Baptist

That he would be poor and needy, Psalm 40 tells us. Jesus said that while the foxes have holes and the birds have nests, the Son of Man has nowhere to lay his head. Psalm 78 says he would speak in parables. Psalm 107 says that he would be One who would still the storms. Zechariah 9:1 explains the triumphal entry of our Lord. Isaiah 53, Psalm 69 says he would be despised, rejected, hated without cause. Isaiah 8 says he would be rejected by the Jews.

Tetelestai. All of these are done. All of these have been fulfilled in Christ. All of these prophecies going back a thousand years and more, all the way back to the promise given to man in the Garden of Eden, all of these fulfilled in Christ. Indeed, it is completed.

From Moses to the prophets, Jesus fulfilled every requirement of the law and every prophecy concerning the Messiah. From Micah's prophecy of Bethlehem's infant who would have the government on his shoulder to Isaiah's graphic prediction of the servant by whose stripes we are healed, he has fulfilled them all.

He is the antitype of the brazen serpent in the wilderness. The Passover Lamb whose blood guards the faithful against the angel of death. He Himself is the faithful High Priest moving now on the Day of Atonement—the genuine Day of Atonement—to the holy place to make a once-for-all sacrifice for sin. All this is summarized and contained in that simple exclamation, "It is finished." Hebrews 7:25: "Consequently, he is able to save to the uttermost those who draw near to God through him, since he always lives to make intercession for them."

Still, we wonder, *Is there something else that draws all of this together?* Some other word that perhaps we can use to give expression to this, "It is finished"? This word which Jesus has used, *tetelestai*, is there some way we can explain this word that summarizes all of this prophetic fulfillment and the mediating work of Christ as Jesus, our great High Priest, goes into the holy place? Perhaps that word is *atonement* because atonement has reference to both the one making atonement and the ones in need of atonement.

In Leviticus and in Numbers, the Jews are taught that they were required once a year, and in addition to the daily sacrifices, to observe a Day of Atonement. What made this day unique is that the priest wouldn't wear his usual high priestly robe which would have gold and was very ornamental. Instead, he bathe from head to toe, and wash himself, and change into a robe that was all white to represent perfect purity, the perfect purity the sacrifices themselves required.

That is why we read in Zechariah that when Joshua's filthy clothes are removed from him, and he was re-clothed with clean clothes, God said, "I have caused your iniquity to pass away," symbolically removing defilement and putting onto him righteousness and holiness. In Ezekiel and Daniel, those who stand near to God are dressed in white to represent purity.

On the Day of Atonement in the history of Israel, a bull was offered as a sin offering for the priest because the priest himself had to have a sacrifice for sin. Then two goats were brought forward. One of the goats would be sacrificed for the sins of the people. And then a very interesting ceremony was performed where the sins of the people were confessed by the priest's laying his hands on the head of the second goat, and the second goat would then be led out to the wilderness and released into the wilderness.

So one goat was sacrificed with the blood serving as an offering for sin. And then the other would serve as a scapegoat to take the sins away. While the details of the celebration of the Day of Atonement are instructive and would be engaging for us to cover in detail, I want us to hold onto these key ideas: the symbolism of the purity of the priest's garments, the sacrifice of the goat for sin, and the symbolic removal of sin in the scapegoat because Christ has performed all of these in his life and on the Cross on the great Day of Atonement for all of God's people.

As our Priest, Jesus kept perfectly the law of God, and so he was pure. There was not a bull that had to be offered to make him right ritualistically to present the sacrifice before the Lord. First Peter 3:18: "Christ also suffered once for sins, the righteous for the unrighteous, that he might bring us to God." Christ the righteous suffered for the sins of the unrighteous—that would be you and me.

With the fall of man and our sin of rebellion against God came the curse of eternal separation from God—the death after death. But Jesus became the sin offering and the scapegoat on the Day of Atonement. If all this means that the work of atonement is completed, then there is nothing we can do. There is nothing more that can be added to what has already been done. There isn't a ritual we can perform that would add to or increase the power of his atonement.

The nature and completeness of Christ's atonement becomes and remains one of the major divisions between the Protestant and the Roman Church of today. The confessions, the committals, and the purgatory of Rome all signal a conviction that the atonement was only partial, that the propitiation for sin was not complete, and that there remains yet a work for us to do. This idea that more is needed is displayed in the mass even in which the sacrifice of Christ is reenacted day after day.

Our conviction is that the Scripture teaches the atonement was complete, that our salvation comes from our being found in Christ rather than from our own perfection through works. So Hebrews teaches us in chapter 9, verse 11 and following. "But when Christ appeared as a high priest of the good things that have come . . . he entered once for all into the holy places, not by means of the blood of goats and calves but by means of His own blood, thus securing an eternal redemption." And so it is that sinners, justly under the sentence of death, are rescued and declared holy.

As Krummacher observed, "Yes, by the one act of the offering up of himself, he has so laid the foundation for all who believe in him of their justification, sanctification, and redemption."[5] With the word from the Lord, "It is finished," all the fullness of our deliverance and transmission to heaven was completed. God has given us these four evidences of the finished work of Christ.

Firstly, *the veil was torn in half*, showing that our access to God was no longer blocked, but that the way was open. That is, the veil between the holy place and the holy of holies. Secondly, *God has given us the resurrection*, proving that the work of Christ, that is, his active obedience, his perfect righteousness, and his passive obedience as the sacrifice for sin were accepted and approved by God. So he is the first fruits of our very own resurrection. The first who has been raised from the dead, the One whom we will follow as we are found to be in Christ.

The third proof that God has accepted this proclamation by Jesus that it is completed was *the exaltation of his own Son, Christ, who now is sitting with him at his own right hand*. That proves that God is well pleased with the finished work of his son. And then finally, *Pentecost, the sending of the Holy Spirit*. The establishment of his Church on earth proves the previous state of man had passed and the kingdom of God has arrived.

"It is finished," means all has been done, and we now rest on the finished work of Christ. What can we add to this finished work? Nothing—unless we would ruin it. So we sing a confession of truth when we sing the song,

> Jesus paid it all,
> All to Him I owe;
> Sin had left a crimson stain,
> He washed it white as snow.

Just as Isaiah foretold in 53:6, "The LORD has laid on him the iniquity of us all." Paul affirms the same thing in Romans 6:23, "The free gift of God is eternal life in Christ Jesus our Lord."

---

5. Krummacher, *The Suffering Savior*, 433.

In conclusion, there is a warning which is issued through Scripture and has been taught by A. W. Pink on these very words. He laments that the words of Christ have been misunderstood and have been misapplied to teach that the beneficiaries have no requirement to pursue holiness and live holy lives on earth. While claiming to rest in the finished work of Christ, many live unfruitful lives. They have no reverent fear of the Lord and no attraction to the beauty of his name.

His fulfilling all righteousness didn't destroy righteousness, but established it that we might live in righteousness. It did finish all that is necessary that the children of God would be saved by the satisfaction of God's wrath. And on account of that, let us run the race with endurance. Let us fight the good fight. Let us finish the work he has for us to do.

Jesus paid it all. All to him we owe. And so may we learn from this word, *tetelestai*, that it is complete. It is finished. Our salvation is secure and assured. Let us learn to love the Lord our God with all of our heart, and with all of our soul, and with all of our minds.

18

Pierced

John 19:31-37

> Since it was the day of Preparation, and so that the bodies would not remain on the cross on the Sabbath (for that Sabbath was a high day), the Jews asked Pilate that their legs might be broken and that they might be taken away. So the soldiers came and broke the legs of the first, and of the other who had been crucified with him. But when they came to Jesus and saw that he was already dead, they did not break his legs. But one of the soldiers pierced his side with a spear, and at once there came out blood and water. He who saw it has borne witness—his testimony is true, and he knows that he is telling the truth—that you also may believe. For these things took place that the Scripture might be fulfilled: "Not one of his bones will be broken." And again another Scripture says, 'They will look on him whom they have pierced."

The last section of our Passion narrative relates to us the humiliation of Christ in his burial. The change of scene shows us that the Jews once again went to Pilate; they planned to him to ask that the bodies be removed from the crosses, even if it meant hastening their death. They needed those bodies removed before sunset because sunset marked the official beginning of the Passover celebration, and it also marks the beginning of the burial narrative.

In this, the Jews made a request that was actually contrary to common Roman practice. Rome, as a matter of course, would leave crucified bodies on the cross to be eaten by animals or simply to rot. Death was a pitiless death. There was no pity to be shown to them at all. Sometimes those who were crucified might linger on the cross two or three days suffering.

The Jews, according to Deuteronomy 21, verses 22 and 23, had a law indicating clearly that a body was not to be left after sunset because those who were crucified had the curse of God upon them, and to leave them on the cross would be to defile the whole land once the day had set.

It's an interesting fact that we might note—almost a footnote—in our mind, that the Jewish leadership here is continuing that practice of straining at gnats to get all of the details of their customs correct while they had been content—we might even say perfectly content—to allow everything to include perjury in the trials just hours before. It was just as Spurgeon said, "Religious scruples may live in a dead conscience."[1]

Perhaps their motivation owed to what John Peter Lange describes as, "They doubtless felt a mysterious impulse from an evil conscience which urged them to hurry into the grave the body of Jesus which hung upon the Cross as a living reproach against them that they might, if possible, consign to oblivion both his person and his cause."[2]

Their work and their misdeeds were hanging before the world to see in the person of Jesus. How quickly their thirst which was quenched with victory was now turning again to a parched thirst as their evil conscience began to speak. As they begin to see in Jesus their own infamy before the people, they wanted to do away with not only his cause, but his very person. The quicker they could get that into the grave, the quicker they could get that sealed and out of sight the better.

This is not simply speculation, but human nature. Don't we see the same thing played out in lives today, where people will seek to eliminate the victim or evidence of their misdeeds?

So the Jews went to Pilate. They asked him to employ a practice that is called *crurifragium* to expedite the deaths. It's a brutal method where an iron bar—perhaps it had a heavy anvil or a hammer on the end—but this iron bar would be taken, heavy as it was, lifted by the soldiers, and then brought against the legs or the knees of the crucified.

The purpose of this was to break the legs—sometimes this practice is even listed as a punishment all by itself without crucifixion—but the purpose in breaking their legs was to keep them from being able to push up and relieve pressure on the chest. The result was nearly instant suffocation. If you would remember the position of one who is on the cross, as

---

1. Boice, *The Gospel of John*, 1383.
2. Lange, *The Life of the Lord Jesus Christ*, 330

the body begins to sag, the lungs expand, and it takes a great deal of effort to exhale. And in lifting their body up, they're able to exhale and push air out. And so as the body begins to sag, and the ribcage expands, and the lungs fill up with air, they're unable, as the strength begins to ebb from them, to push with the diaphragm to get the air out to bring fresh air in. So they actually die of suffocation.

Their request was rapidly granted by Pilate. Additional guards were dispatched to carry out the task, probably two, or most likely even three. Two to carry the clubs, and then there would have been a third one with them, the one probably holding the javelin or the spear. They were dispatched to carry out the task, and they began on the sides. Two of them, one on one side, and one on the other. They broke the legs of the two thieves, and then met in the center where Christ was hanging on the Cross. They found him already dead.

The soldiers were most likely glad to be spared the trouble of having to heave that iron bar up one last time to break his legs. It had to be heaved up high. Remember, the crucified were lifted up, so this iron bar would be picked up high, and then swung in a manner which would break the legs. They couldn't leave the work however unless they were absolutely sure that he was in fact dead.

So they took a spear. The soldier thrust the point of the spear into Jesus' side, almost certainly aiming for the heart as he would have been taught when he using the spear in combat. He would have been standing before the Cross, Jesus before him hanging, with the spear thrust most likely into the left side ribcage.

It was a nasty weapon, the spears that they used, with a barbed iron head meant to cause incredible amounts of damage because again the spears would be used in battle. The wound was substantial, and we know that because Thomas would later be invited to put his hand into the place where Jesus' side was pierced. And from that wound we are told flowed both blood and water.

John immediately notes the significance of the event. He notes that Scripture is being fulfilled as blood and water flow from the side of Jesus. First of all, he notes that not a bone of Jesus' body was broken. They were commanded in Exodus 12 that when a Passover lamb was to be presented, not a bone of that lamb can be harmed. Also, Zechariah, chapter 12, verse 10, predicts that Jesus would be pierced.

The Zechariah passage has puzzled Jewish commentators and Jewish teachers for so many years that they actually changed that word *pierced* to the word *despised* in the Greek *Septuagint* so that it would say they would look upon him who was despised rather than the one who was pierced because without any linguistic support in that change, they couldn't imagine that God would be pierced. But God could be despised. And so again, without any linguistic support, those Jews changed the Greek translation of *Septuagint* from *pierced* to *despised*.

Two passages of Scripture given so far apart in time, fulfilled by God's providential leading of a Roman soldier, himself ignorant of the Scriptures. Imagine that! Here the soldier stands only glad to be relieved of having to swing a heavy metal bar and break another's legs. And so he takes a spear as a lighter duty simply to make sure that a Man has already died. And in doing so, God providentially directed that two Scriptures given thousands of years apart would be fulfilled in that single act at the Cross of Christ.

John had a view of Jesus that emphasized him as the true Paschal Lamb in his teaching. He mentions this about Jesus on several occasions. When the Jews selected a lamb for the Passover, they had to take the lamb into their home for three days, identifying with that lamb, feeling some sympathy for the lamb. And on the third day, it was killed. But not a single bone of that lamb could be broken. Jesus fulfilled the picture of the true Paschal Lamb completely.

Perhaps even more startling is the prophecy of Zechariah 12 however. In Zechariah 12, the Lord breaks the backs of Israel's stronger enemies when Israel herself was not able to defeat them in battle. Then he breaks the hearts of his people, causing them to repent of their enmity against him. Forgiveness. They then strive to attain satisfaction by removing everything wicked and ungodly.

God grants to them a forgiveness, and then the people begin to strive for sanctification, removing ungodliness. We often refer to this as the mortification of the flesh. We are forgiven by the atoning blood of Jesus Christ, and then our lives are spent in the process of sanctification, the mortification of the sin out of the body.

In that prophetic vision, Israel aimed a deadly thrust at that Man who would come to represent God before the people; Israel would hate that Man. Zechariah prophesies that they will be compelled in the end however to look upon him whom they pierced. Piercing signified their hate of God's highest manifestation and approach to them. And the prophecy was that they would learn to regret their action. As Revelation 1:7 shows, "Every eye will see him, even those who pierced him."

And so we find this connectivity and this consistency all throughout the Scriptures. In Zechariah, it talks of those who will pierce the Lord's representative, those who will be made to look upon him. And then in Revelation 1, we will see that fulfillment that "every eye will see him, even those who pierced him." We have this connection sovereignly made between the law of Moses and the prophecy of Zechariah.

Beyond this, John identifies another sign, that of blood and water flowing from our Savior's side. So we have here two signs given to John. One, the prophetic fulfillment, and two, the actual blood and the water. James Montgomery Boice identifies three wrong interpretations of the blood and the water. There is a great deal of speculation, and if you've heard much variety in preaching on this particular passage, you may have heard several different approaches to the blood and the water.

The first one that will be mentioned—and in fact, this one has some heavy weight support for accepting it—is that the blood and the water would signify the two sacraments of the Church. That is, the Eucharist, or the Lord's Supper, and baptism. Nothing else in the gospels however supports that view, but many—to include Augustine, and Roman exegetes of the ancient Church, and Martin Luther himself—advocated this view.

There was also a view advocated that the wound in Christ's side was like the door in the side of the ark—the ark itself representing the Church—and that it was from that door that animals would go into safety and be saved. Another says that as Adam fell asleep and that Eve was brought from his side, so Jesus when he bowed his head, in essence fell asleep, and that it was the Church that was born from his side.

John never makes these connections in any of his teaching. In fact, if we were to look over in 1 John, chapter 5, verses 6 and 7, "This is he who came by water and blood—Jesus Christ; not by the water only but by the water and the blood. And the Spirit is the one who testifies, because the Spirit is the truth. For there are three that testify."

So even here, John does make mention of water and of blood, but he doesn't make it in connection with the birth of the Church. He doesn't make any connection with the sacraments of the Church. Some argue, that since Eve came out of the side of Adam, that the Church was also born from the side of Christ. But this really has no support in Scripture either. And in fact, this view does damage to covenantal theology.

Others believe this proves Jesus died of a broken heart. Sentimentally, this has a great deal of appeal, and certainly Jesus was moved by his act of atonement. Some believe that medical evidence points to his having a broken heart because of the effusion of fluid into the pericardium, the thin sac around the heart.

But if that were the case, they've also shown medically that if a spear were thrust into the side, and it did penetrate that sac, instead of flowing out from the wound, that fluid would actually fill the chest cavity. So any biological support for that view simply fails.

Men such as Swedenborg insisted that the blood signifies divine truth for the spiritual man, and the water signifies divine truth for the natural man. Again, while this has good scriptural tones and sounds, it simply finds no support in Scripture. Others suggest that the whole purpose was simply to prove that Jesus was real flesh and blood, that he had a real body, and wasn't simply a phantom as Docetism claims.

You remember in our study of 1 John that Docetic influence was something that John was battling against. But again we don't find the other scriptural support for this view. Others feel that it was to prove Jesus really died, that he didn't just swoon or faint as some would claim. Proponents of this view say that he was placed unconscious into the tomb, and from the tomb he woke up because of the coolness. This again denies the whole incarnation and atonement.

John never calls on the event to make such proofs. The water and the blood bear a different testimony. In his view, this event has a far greater importance than strictly literal, pragmatic, or scientific explanations. The thrust of the spear summarized the whole crucifixion, the whole of man's hatred. And so the sign of Christ, the eternal Temple of God, came with it.

Blood and water have long been a part of Jewish and Christian theology and practice. In the Tabernacle, a worshiper entered the court and was faced with an altar, an altar where there would be the shedding of blood. There was a requirement for cleansing from sin, and then after passing past the altar, they would approach the brazen laver, a purification from uncleanness by the water that was in the laver was required.

The blood of Jesus is the basis of spiritual life in every believer. Water is symbolic of cleansing of life of the spirit. Deliverance and cleansing from the defilement of sin is the result of Christ's work on the Cross and the testimony of his blood and water. It also reflects the teaching of the prophecy of Zechariah, which this makes a direct connection to.

We've sung of this often in the testimony of our hymns, such as *Rock of Ages*.

> Rock of Ages, cleft for me,
> Let me hide myself in Thee;
> Let the water and the blood,
> From Thy riven side which flowed,
> Be of sin the double cure,
> Save from wrath and make me pure.

Or another:

> There is a fountain filled with blood,
> Drawn from Immanuel's veins,
> And sinners plunged beneath that flood
> Lose all their guilty stains.

While the Cross has supplanted forever the altar of sacrifices, you wonder about the water of the laver that you hold in your hand. I speak now of the Scriptures. What is it practically speaking that can have the same impact and the same affect on our lives as that laver where priest would wash before going into the holy place?

In Ephesians, chapter 5, we read that "Christ loved the church and gave himself up for her, that he might sanctify her, having cleansed her by the washing of water with the word." By the power and work of the Spirit of Christ that is present in us, the washing of water with the word continues to have its affect.

From the fulfilling of prophecy to the promise of salvation and sanctification, the lame, the poor all serve the purposes of God just as the lance and the spear served his purpose. Do you have the blood of the Passover Lamb on your door that death, the final death, will pass you by? Do you hear the Spirit of Christ in his Word so that it has the effect of completing the work which God has begun in you? Did you flow from the Savior's side? Did that flow reach you? Are you washed in the blood of the Lamb?

19

Buried with the King

John 19:38-42

> After these things Joseph of Arimathea, who was a disciple of Jesus, but secretly for fear of the Jews, asked Pilate that he might take away the body of Jesus, and Pilate gave him permission. So he came and took away his body. Nicodemus also, who earlier had come to Jesus by night, came bringing a mixture of myrrh and aloes, about seventy-five pounds in weight. So they took the body of Jesus and bound it in linen cloths with the spices, as is the burial custom of the Jews. Now in the place where he was crucified there was a garden, and in the garden a new tomb in which no one had yet been laid. So because of the Jewish day of Preparation, since the tomb was close at hand, they laid Jesus there.

Have you ever cared a great deal about something when it was too late to do anything about it? Have you ever thought as you've gotten older that you wish you had eaten a little bit better when you were younger? Have you ever reflected back on your years of school and thought that perhaps if you had paid a little bit more attention or maybe spent just a few moments studying this subject or that that it would have been a great benefit for you later on? Have you ever had a damaged relationship in your life, and you waited until it was too late to wish that you had reconciled?

I have recently had a member of my high school who passed away—no one whom I was close with, but I was startled to learn that she had died. I didn't know she was sick. I'd never even seen her actually since graduation. Yet something inside me wanted to go to the funeral or speak to the family because it seemed such a tragedy that someone had passed away whom I had once known, even casually.

Somehow I felt that something should have been said somewhere along the way. I don't know what. It was just a feeling, and it struck me that that is often the way it goes with us. We don't think about speaking until we no longer can.

Two matters are before us in the passage for this chapter: first of all, the continuing and the concluding humiliation of Christ, and then secondly, the immediacy of genuine and true discipleship. What sadness must the tiny band of disciples at the foot of the Cross been experiencing. It was around four in the afternoon, perhaps even later. Our Lord had died. He had breathed his last, and they were there mourning his loss.

Among them was this one Joseph of Arimathea. Perhaps Nicodemus was there. Perhaps he joined later. We haven't been introduced to Joseph of Arimathea previously. In the gospels, the synoptics, Matthew emphasizes that Joseph was wealthy, that he was a disciple. Luke tells us that Joseph was a man of high character and stresses that he didn't agree with the counsel that convicted Jesus. He may have been excluded from the trial because they just didn't give him an invitation perhaps being suspicious of his sympathies or perhaps he determined not to attend because he didn't want to participate in this sort of a court. It's fairly certain he wasn't a part of the trial because all who were there gave their consent.

Absent at the trial, now he seems to be trying to make amends. Luke mentions that Joseph was a man who was looking for the kingdom of God. Mark also mentions Joseph's hope for the kingdom of God and his position on the Sanhedrin. John, on the other hand, neglects to mention his wealth. He doesn't mention his membership on the Sanhedrin and his searching for the kingdom of God. Instead, John wants to emphasize for us the secrecy of his affections for Christ and his fear of being found out that he was one who listened to Christ.

He is introduced to us as a certain Joseph, a character who was held in reserve until just this moment. The burial would not be a family burial for Jesus, but one by a disciple, and in effect through this disciple, one of the Church, as Christ is now a part of his disciples and a part of the Church, fulfilling the prophecy of Isaiah 53:9, "And they made his grave with the wicked and with a rich man in his death, although he had done no violence, and there was no deceit in his mouth."

Ordinarily, the bodies of criminals would be given to the family except in cases of sedition. In those cases where one was accused of sedition and then crucified, they were piled together in a mass grave somewhere outside of the city. In the case of Jesus, even if the family had been allowed to take the body, they, because of their station in life, would never have been given access to Pilate to ask. But as one sovereignly reserved by God for this very time, this wealthy, well-respected member of the Sanhedrin was given an audience with Pilate.

How odd Pilate's day must have been. He started that morning unsuspicious of all that would occur that day in human history and the part he would play in that day. He was first petitioned by the Sanhedrin, but he had to go out to them because they couldn't come in to him for fear of becoming unclean. How ironic that they ask a man for help in their schemes but could not enter his dwelling for fear of being unclean.

Against his wife's best advice, Pilate accepted the case and became involved in a strange series of events and a judgment that condemned a Man whom he himself believed to be innocent. He became embarrassed by the Jews' manipulation, by those who would be his subjects—those same members of the Sanhedrin who would come back later to ask Pilate to hasten the death of Jesus because of their religious sensitivities about the Passover.

To his surprise, Jesus was already dead. He had died quickly, more quickly than had been anticipated. And now a member of the Sanhedrin wanted to take custody of Jesus and bury Him honorably at his own personal expense! For Pilate, this was an appropriate ending to the entire affair. The One hated by the Sanhedrin whom they had wanted so desperately to crucify would now be honored in the end by one of their own counsel.

John tells us that Joseph was not alone however in taking care of the body of Jesus. Nicodemus helped. We have met Nicodemus on a couple of occasions. We met him in John, chapter 3. He came to Jesus in the secrecy of darkness. He was also looking for the kingdom, we're told. And Jesus told him, "Unless one is born again he cannot see the kingdom of God."

Perhaps both were present when the Pharisees asked Jesus when the kingdom would come, and maybe they heard Christ's answer to them when he said, "The kingdom of God is not coming with signs to be observed, nor will they say, 'Look, here it is!' or 'There!' for behold, the kingdom of God is in the midst of you." Perhaps that was their draw to Christ. Perhaps they somehow understood he embodied the very kingdom of God, still mysterious to them, but yet maybe they had heard his words, and maybe they were seeking to understand this One Jesus Christ.

But to this point, their secrecy had been as great a denial of Christ as Peter's own denial. And by seeking to make so great an amends, weren't they actually denying the resurrection itself? In seeking to make such grand preparations for burial, did they mention any expectation of his rising again? They seemed to be trying to make amends for their lack, for their absence, for their lack of support, their lack of voice, their not speaking up for Christ in a time of crises. They were making a grand funeral for this One whom they had come to know, whom they had come to love in their own way, and yet had not stood for.

Neither of the two men are mentioned in any records of a first century church. We have no real assurance that they ever actually came to any saving knowledge of Christ. Perhaps they did. Perhaps they did not.

Where were these two men, now doing such a great service to Jesus, when he himself was walking among men? Where was their great love of Christ when he taught in the courts of the Temple? Where were they when he was faced by the Pharisees' questions? These two men for fear of losing their reputation remained silent and secret disciples. John had already mentioned men like these in chapter 12, saying, "They loved the glory that comes from man more than the glory that comes from God."

Discipleship is never something you can decide to do later. When a rich man asked Jesus how he could be saved, Jesus called him to forsake everything and to follow him right then. In Mark, chapter 8, verse 34, when speaking to a crowd, Jesus said to them, "If anyone would come after me, let him deny himself and take up his cross and follow me. For whoever would save his life will lose it, but whoever loses his life for my sake and the gospel's will save it."

In Luke, chapter 9, verse 26, we find added to this, "For whoever is ashamed of me and of my words, of him will the Son of Man be ashamed." Even when in Luke 9:60 a man requested a delay to care for his dying parents that he might honor them with burial, Jesus said, "Leave the dead to bury their own dead. But as for you, go and proclaim the kingdom of God." He even says that there is no time to go back and say goodbye to those at home because "No one who puts his hand to the plow and looks back is fit for the kingdom of God."

Discipleship carries a cost for *every* disciple, every one without exception. One Joseph and Nicodemus had not yet been willing to pay because they were held in check by fear—by fear of their identification with Christ. But John does make a strong case that Joseph, even if it was late, acted with great courage.

Courage is a catalyst to make real any other supposed or cherished virtue we might imagine we possess. Love cannot be trusted until it's proven. That is why so many young people are tricked as they first experience emotional attraction to one another. They truly believe they are in love, but a love not tested is a love not proved. Fidelity isn't certain until we have been tempted by infidelity and have turned it back. Courage proves or disproves a character.

A character is something that can be studied, but until it is authenticated by action, courageously sacrificing to preserve a character, to preserve in our case discipleship and faithfulness, it has not been proved to be true. Hence, we can know, but not know.

Perhaps this is the moment for Joseph and Nicodemus when they were walking from darkness to light. Whether they were born again or not, they waited until the last moment. At the point when nothing can be done to prevent Jesus from dying, they offer their help.

Is your own discipleship a courageous discipleship, or is it a safe discipleship? Is it a casual, cowardly discipleship? Is your own walk of faith—the one you are in now—active in your pursuit of God's kingdom, or are you waiting, much like funeral directors, for the end to come when then, and only then, it would be safe to step up and say, "Oh I was with you all along in spirit"? Will you be filled with remorse for missed opportunities in which could have labored for Christ and for his kingdom? Is your life an open, living confession of Christ? Do you hear him? Do you teach of him? Do you proclaim him and love him before others, or are your lips sealed as you wander through your days?

Are you a disciple in your own mind, or are you a disciple in the activities of your life? Are you a secret disciples, secure only in your own imagination and self-delusion of the authenticity of your love for Christ—an authenticity that cannot be proved, for you turn down every opportunity, always waiting until tomorrow to serve, always waiting until the next time to give your all to Christ? Are you a soldier of Christ, or are you simply a visitor in his courts?

Why do those who profess Christ deny him with their lives? John explains—it's fear. Fear and vanity. People today seek lives, even religious lives—remember, these were members of the Sanhedrin—religious lives that impress others. Joseph and Nicodemus were both well thought of.

They were both serving on the highest religious court in the world, the Sanhedrin, God's people's court. They had good reputation there. They served faithfully. They had all the accoutrements of their religion. They knew their Scriptures, and yet their discipleship faltered.

People today seek lives, even religious lives, that mirror the same thing. What keeps you from serving Jesus who is King and who is now reigning in his kingdom? For wherever the rule of God commands the hearts of men, there is the kingdom of God.

What about this other attendant at Christ's burial, this other one with Joseph—Nicodemus? He brought the myrrh and the aloes, nearly a hundred pounds. Because they were wealthy, they would have had servants, and undoubtedly their servants would have helped them with the load and with the handling of Christ's body. Because they were men of means, they had the resources and they had the help, and the servants would not only help carry the spices, but help to very gingerly and gently remove the spikes and the nails from the feet of Christ, and then to take the cross member from that Cross, and to gently lower that to the ground where then they could remove them from his hands.

The grave itself was most likely located only about 45 yards away if current estimations are correct. But the hour was growing late, and the sun was very near setting. Joseph and Nicodemus must have coordinated with one another ahead of time because everything was prepared. The tomb was prepared. The spices were prepared. The servants were ready to go. He already knew what he would do when he went to Joseph to get the body. He knew just where to take it. There was no delay. They must have planned the burial before the actual crucifixion.

Laying his body either on a makeshift table or on the ground, they sprinkled the spices on Jesus. After ceremonially cleaning off any of the dried blood and cleaning his body, they wrapped him in layers of cloth, adding more spices as they with each layer. The preparation of the Jews was not like the embalming of the Egyptians. The Egyptians would soak a body for 70 days in order to mummify it, but the Jews internment was more of a consecration for the transition or the translation of a body from life to dust.

With the sun continuing to set, always looking to check and make sure they were still within the time limits that they had, the preparations moved fast and without a eulogy. Without the glory that he had known, the Lord was quietly put away by those who did not yet understand him.

His tomb was sealed. It grew silent. And the people who were there to help prepare him began to make their way back to their homes even as lights were beginning to be lit in the windows of those houses.

In darkness he lay—a noble Man, yet unknown as the incarnate and the true God among them. Never, never was Jesus less known than he was when the tomb was sealed. Here was the final chapter of a humiliation of Christ. The Westminster Larger Catechism in question 46 explains his humiliation well. We can do no better. "The estate of Christ's humiliation was that low condition, wherein he for our sakes, emptying himself of his glory, took upon him the form of a servant, in his conception and birth, life, death, and after his death, until his resurrection."

Now consider again your own courage and your service to the risen Christ as you reflect on his gifts to you. His life for yours. Your suffering placed upon him. Your death which he died. And you are afraid to speak for him? Why? What would cause you to hesitate? What would cause you to not give your all except fear or vanity?

It's a sad record that Joseph and Nicodemus shared fellowship with Christ only after he died. Imagine that they might have walked with Christ for three years, that they could have heard every parable, witnessed every miracle. They could have listened to every sermon. They could have talked with the other disciples and considered all of the ideas. They could have explored all of their hopes for the kingdom with the One who had the answers to all of their questions.

But instead, they forfeited their fellowship with Christ to keep their pre-Christian lives intact. A secret disciple will always lose fellowship with Christ because every moment of every day is a decision to follow or to walk away. They neglect their duties. They neglect the testimonies. And so the distance from Christ will grow greater. It's that way with any relationship.

Consider your relationship within your own homes. If you're always choosing to spend your time elsewhere, what happens with the relationship within the home? Consider your relationship with your church. If you absent yourself from your church, where will the relationship grow stronger—with your church body or without? Consider any relationship you have, whether it is with your children when they leave home, whether it's with your spouse, whether it is with your church family, or with Christ. When you choose to walk in a different direction and spend your days in a place other than walking with Christ, how can you expect your discipleship to grow stronger?

But perhaps there is an encouragement. It is the death of Christ that brought these secret disciples out. When other disciples had fled, these two disciples stepped forward and did provide from their own accounts for the care of the body of Christ. Was this their awakening? Was this their moment of understanding? Did they feel the guilt of their past abandonment of their duties to Christ? It took his death, but at long last, at least now they had identified themselves with him.

Now for us. The shadows are growing long as the end of days are drawing near. If not in human history, if we will not be here for the final consummation of the kingdom as Christ descends from the heavens with a shout, then at least in our own lives the shadows are beginning to draw long. The Lord has suffered much for his own, and he has given not only life, but a mission.

What will it take to move you and to move me into the cause of Christ? What will bring you out of the shadows, as Joseph and Nicodemus were finally brought out of the shadows and into his service? What will remove your excuses and your insecurities and call you to immediate action? The Lord has not asked; he has commanded that you follow him. It's not a favor; it's an act of obedience, an act of faith. Have you? Some have. Will you? Some will.

Unless you are the perfect disciple, which there will never be one in this flesh, unless you have perfectly walked with Christ, there is always a better walk. There is always more love. There is always more testimony. There is always more seeking. There is always a turning back to Christ. "The Spirit and the Bride say, 'Come.' And let the one who hears say, 'Come.' And let the one who is thirsty come; let the one who desires take the water of life without price."

Bibliography

Barclay, William. *The Gospel of John*. Vol. 2. Philadelphia: Westminster, 1956.
Boice, James Montgomery. *The Gospel of John*. Vol. 5. Grand Rapids: Baker, 1999.
Calvin, John. *Commentary on the Gospel of John*. Vol. 2. Grand Rapids: Baker, 1993.
Dodd, C. H. *The Parables of the Kindgom*. 7th ed. London Nisbet & Co., 1946.
Doyle, Arthur Conan. *Bartlett's Familiar Quotations*. Boston: Little Brown, 1982.
Gorman, Ralph. *The Last Hours of Jesus*. New York: Sheed and Ward, 1960.
Hendrickson, William. *Exposition of the Gospel According to John*. Grand Rapids: Baker, 1976.
Henry, Matthew. *Matthew Henry's Commentary*. Vol. 5. Peabody, MA: Hendrickson, 1991.
Ironside, H. A. *Addresses on the Gospel of John*. 6th ed. New York: Loizeaux Bros., 1956.
Johnston, Graham. *Preaching to a Postmodern World*. Vol. 9. Grand Rapids: Baker, 2001.
Krummacher, Friedrich. *The Suffering Savior: Meditations on the Last Days of Christ*. Chicago: Moody Press, 1947.
Lange, John Peter. *A Commentary on the Holy Scriptures: Critical, Doctrinal and Homiletical*. Vol. 3. New York: Charles Scribner, & Co., 1865.
———. *The Life of the Lord Jesus Christ: A Complete Critical Exam*. Vol. 3. Grand Rapids: Zondervan, 1958.
Martindale, Wayne. *The Quotable C.S. Lewis*. Carol Stream, IL: Tyndale House, 1990.
Phillips, John. *Exploring People of the New Testament*. Grand Rapids: Kregel, 2007.
Pink, Arthur W. *The Seven Sayings of the Savior on the Cross*. Grand Rapids: Baker, 1958.
Ridderbos, Herman. *The Gospel According to John: A Theological Commentary*. Grand Rapids: Eerdmans, 1997.
Rochefoucauld, Francois De La *Bartlett's Familiar Quotations*. Edited by Justin Kaplan. Boston: Little, Brown and Company, 1992.
Schilder, Klass. *Christ on Trial*. Grand Rapids: Eerdmans, 1939.
———. *Christ Crucified*. Grand Rapids: Eerdmans, 1939.
St. Augustine. *Nicene & Post Nicene Fathers*. Vol. 7. Grand Rapids: Eerdmans, 2002.
Tennyson, Alfred Lord. *Century Dictionary*. Vol. 7. Edited by William Dwight Whitney and Benjamin Eli Smith. New York: Century, 1906.
Thatcher, Margaret. *American Reference Books Annual, 1985-1989*. Cambridge : Harvard Univeristy Press, 1989.
Tullus, Marcus. Quoted in Josef Blinzler, *The Trial of Jesus*. Newman Press: Westminster, 1959.

www.ingramcontent.com/pod-product-compliance
Lightning Source LLC
Chambersburg PA
CBHW051932160426
43198CB00012B/2121